HAWAII: THE SUGAR-COATED FORTRESS

HAWAII: THE SUGAR-COATED FORTRESS

Francine du Plessix Gray

Random House · *New York*

All the material in this book appeared originally in *The New Yorker*.

All rights reserved under International and Pan-American Copyright
Conventions. Published in the United States by Random House, Inc.,
New York, and simultaneously in Canada by Random House of Canada
Limited, Toronto.
Library of Congress Cataloging in Publication Data

Gray, Francine du Plessix.
Hawaii: the sugar-coated fortress.
1. Hawaii—History.   2. Hawaii—Politics and
government—1959-   3. Hawaii—Race question.
4. Hawaii—Economic conditions—1918-   I. Title.
DU625.G66   1972   320.9'969   77–37042
ISBN 0–394–47979–3

Manufactured in the United States of America
by Haddon Craftsmen, Scranton, Pa.
9 8 7 6 5 4 3 2

To my sons, Thaddeus and Luke Gray,
and to a generation demanding peace

The dignity and beauty of man rests in the human spirit which makes him more than simply a physical being. This spirit must never be suppressed for exploitation by others. As long as the people recognize the beauty of their human spirits and move against suppression and exploitation, they will be carrying out one of the most beautiful ideas of all time. Because the human whole is much greater than the sum of its parts.

—Huey P. Newton

ACKNOWLEDGMENTS

During the months I spent in Hawaii researching this essay, the friendship and aid of James and Page Foster were most precious to me. I am indebted to them for their loving thoughtfulness and hospitality, and for the constant warmth which they infused into our stay on the islands.

I am equally indebted to Robin Foster for his meticulous help in researching this work, which was originally conceived as a profile for *The New Yorker* magazine. Its completion would have been most difficult without Robin Foster's imaginative and vigorous assistance.

Special gratitude also to Kalani Ohelo, Senator Vince Yano, John Witeck and Wayne Hayashi—gratitude for their friendship, which I value greatly, and equal gratitude for helping me to grasp the most urgent contemporary issues of reform and justice facing Hawaiians.

For helping me to discern the deeper meaning of the Hawaiian past, so much of it unchronicled, I am profoundly obliged to John Dominis Holt. I look upon him as the spiritual mentor of this book.

I am thankful also to Dr. Sam Elbert, Dr. Terence Barrow and to Jean and Zohmah Charlot for their invaluable insights into Hawaiian culture, and for their generosity in sharing them with me.

My gratitude to the following islanders for their advice and hospitality: Walter and Betty Johnson, John and Aiko Reinecke, Harriet Bouslog and Steve Sawyer, Duke and Mary Choy, Willis and Barbara Butler, Frederick and Joanne Trotter, James and Leila Morgan, Tom and Connie Dinnell, James Shingle, Bernice and Emmet Cahill, Joseph and Alice Feher, Asa Baber, Atherton Richards, Monsignor Daniel Dever, Michael and Sheila Forman, William Abbott, Selden and Barbara Washington, the Reverend Richard Kirckhoffer, the Reverend Larry Jones, the Reverend Claude DuTeil.

I would also like to thank the following persons for interrupting their work to speak to me on many Hawaiian issues, past and present, cultural and political: Governor John Burns, Congresswoman Patsy Mink, Congressman Spark Matsunaga, Tony Hodges, Dr. Alan Howard, Dr. Ronald Gallimore, Dr. Jan Newhouse, Dr. Edward Beechert, Howard Miyake, Tom Gill, Dr. Harlan Cleveland, Dr. Thomas Hamilton, Fred Cachola, Hung Wo Ching, Hung Wai Ching, Monsignor Charles Kekumano, the Reverend Abraham Akaka, Randy Kalahiki, John and Marion Kelly, Dr. Roland Force, Senator Hiram Fong, Myron Thompson, Fuifatu Fau'olo, George Chaplin, Herman Doi, Bob Dye, Mayor Frank Fasi, Dr. Katharine Luomala, Herbert Takahashi, Pae Galdeira, Soli Niheu, Mayor Shunichi Kimura, Dr. Linus Pauling, Jr., Brook Hart, David Thompson, Robert and A.Q. McElrath, Henry Walker, Jr., Malcolm Mac Naughton, Allen Wilcox, Chinn Ho, Steve Murin, Dr. James Dator, Dr. Gavan Daws, Dr. Thomas Hitch, Dr. Norman Meller, Yasuki and Florence Arakaki, Mrs. Taylor A. Pryor, William and Philippa Reich,

Dr. James Douglass, Dr. Gregory Bateson, Colonel Young O. Kim, and Mrs. Doris Jivenden of the U. S. Army Public Information Office.

Two outstanding historical works which should be read by anyone traveling to our fiftieth state—Gavan Daws' *Shoal of Time* and Lawrence Fuchs' *Hawaii Pono*—provided much background for my research. I am indebted to their excellence and to their authors, and I am particularly grateful to Dr. Daws for reading through a major part of my manuscript for historical accuracy.

Finally, a special word of thanks to my friend Gerardo Jovinelli, whose generosity evidences that even Neapolitan hospitality—however uprooted—can thrive in the most hospitable state of the Union.

HAWAII: THE SUGAR-COATED FORTRESS

I

"**W**elcome to paradise!" the announcer's voice says on the car radio. Flanked by a flare of scarlet plumeria trees and of gold primaveras, a highway sign says PEARL HARBOR, 7 MILES. I am driving through the capital of our fiftieth state with a Hawaiian student dressed in a brown beret and a black leather jacket, in emulation of the mainland's Young Lords. There is a swell of swooning, saccharine music on the radio, followed again by the ebullient disk jockey's voice: "Aloha to paradise!"

"Aloha to the Pentagon of the Pacific," the young Hawaiian mutters.

"What does 'aloha' mean, Kalani?"

"Hello, thank you, good-bye; mostly these days good-bye."

"How did you feel about statehood in '59, Kalani?"

"I was nine years old and I knew it was a bummer."

"What's your solution?"

"Simple. Secede."

Kalani hands me a booklet published by a youth congress whose delegates, representing over thirty Hawaii high schools and colleges, voted in April 1970 to secede from the United States. A quote from their resolution:

We, the Youth Congress family, see that secession from the United States of America will be a catalyst to the preservation of Hawaii's land, culture and people. The Westernization, Americanization and colonization of Hawaii has left in its wake pollution, congestion, ugliness on our land; has inflicted economic slavery upon our people, and has disrupted our culture through the domination of American culture. . . We, as this Youth Congress, must resolve to take all steps necessary to facilitate the secession of Hawaii from the United States of America.

"What happens if you can't secede, Kalani?"

"Possible violence," Kalani says. "Hey, here come the surf reports."

"Waikiki two feet," the announcer's voice drones, "Haleiwa six feet and fair, Makapuu is breaking at three to four feet and good form . . ."

"That," says Kalani, turning away from revolution, "makes it perfect for body surfing."

Honolulu's Ala Moana is the world's largest shopping center, a fifty-acre complex of one hundred and sixty shops steeped in soothing music and warm odors of food and flowers. Open seven days a week and often until midnight, continually seething with humanity, Ala Moana is a gigantic *souk*, a Brucknerian hymn to American consumerism, a perpetual world's fair. At Ala Moana, Polynesian, Japanese, Chinese, and American-style lunch counters alternate with

banks, jewelry stores, tourist agencies, art galleries, Woolworth's, J.C. Penney's, beauty parlors, pet shops, photogra-
phy salons, Dunkin' Donut stands, souvenir booths, muumuu
boutiques, cracked-seed stores, vast emporiums of Japanese,
Tahitian, Indian and other Pacific artifacts. Families gather
for meals on Ala Moana's benches and sculpture-ornamented
walkways to eat their paper-platefuls of tempura and raw
fish, or *poi,* or chow mein, or hot dogs. "Thank you" is written in Hawaiian *(Mahalo)* on the streamlined cobalt-blue
trash cans of Ala Moana's sidewalks; Japanese calligraphy,
alongside Western print, indicates the entrances of rest
rooms; T-shirts selling in the sportswear shops bear the slogan "Visit Saigon, Fun Capital of the World"; the sign "20%
discount to military" is frequently seen. Ala Moana has the
largest Sears Roebuck store in the world; an eight-thousand-
car parking lot; automatic stairways linking its three levels;
mosaics, marbles and bronzes in its fountain courtyards;
pools filled with bloated, somnolent carp; and one of the only
four bookstores in the state of Hawaii, where one can occa-
sionally find a month-old copy of the Sunday *New York
Times.* It is at its most festive every Friday, the state's Aloha
Day, which an association of Hawaiian garment manufactur-
ers has designated as the day for floor-length muumuus. Supermarket attendants, housewives, post-office employees,
bank clerks and schoolteachers are moving columns of flowered cloth, are hung with real or plastic leis of carnations,
orchids, ginger, jasmine. Floral women waft through Ala
Moana's alleys, their long clothes incongruous in full sunlight,
and amidst them drift barefoot, bikini-clad teenagers carry-

ing surfboards under their arms, their bodies still dripping
from the ocean a block away.

Ala Moana's palatial supermarket displays vegetables
Oriental and American, vegetables of monstrous perfection,
vegetables fulfilling the Platonic essence of vegetableness:
string beans eighteen inches long and viridian green, two-
feet-long eggplants, white turnips the size of melons, Chinese cabbages curled and furled like dancers' fans, ginger
roots twisted and ominous as the mandrake's; mounds of
lotus roots, fresh water chestnuts and crystalline bean sprouts
lie alongside gleaming packets of dried seaweed, shredded
mango and fresh bean curd. There is a sense of gigantism, of
glandular excess, of beauty coarsened by abundance. There
is a glut of orchids. Orchids are rampant on the walls of
banks, are treated like parsley sprigs—frilling the bones of
lamb chops at the supermarket; orchids are strewn among
displays of mangos and papayas, are afloat in one's glass of
orange juice, decorate the shrimp cocktail at Woolworth's
lunch counter.

From the upper terrace of Ala Moana's parking lot there
is a vast view of the city of Honolulu, on the south shore of
the island of Oahu, one of the eight major Hawaiian islands
that comprise our fiftieth state. Scores of sugar-white condominiums fleck the violet hulk of Diamond Head crater and
the sumptuous rugged green slopes of the Pali—the cliffs—
behind the city. There are churches in wild profusion, ves-
tiges of a missionary society, of an enormous lottery for souls.
Christopher Wren spires are surreally flanked by coconut
palms and by the crested plumes of the Pali's tropical rain

forest. Brief, delicate spells of rain alternate capriciously with bouts of radiant sunshine, festooning Honolulu with rainbows. Los Angeles-style freeways named after Hawaiian royalty encircle and cross the city, their names rendered childish by the twelve-letter Hawaiian alphabet: Likelike, Lunalilo. There are surfboard racks on the tops of the cars whizzing through Honolulu, like ski racks on a New England winter day.

The city's architecture is as hybrid as the humanity which inhabits it. On its west fringe, a block from the ocean, stands Honolulu's business district, dominated by a gleaming complex of bronzed skyscrapers which calls itself the Financial Plaza of the Pacific. It is adjacent to what remains of Honolulu's Chinatown, a shanty quarter of low clapboard houses where gay bars tended by painted transvestites are flanked by pool halls, massage parlors, skin-flick houses. The state capitol is a lustrous structure in the California-Tokyo style which houses the offices of Governor John Burns, an Irish Catholic former policeman. Across it stands a pale-gray Victorian folly of a building that was briefly the residence of Hawaii's last kings. Two blocks away, next to a luxuriant tropical park which boasts one of the world's largest banyan trees, is City Hall, a beige stucco structure in the Filipino baroque genre presided over by the mayor of Honolulu, a second-generation Italian from Hartford, Connecticut.

Standing at the top of Ala Moana on a Sunday, one is at the nucleus of the city. The streets are clogged with lines of Datsun and Toyota cars all converging, like the rays of a diamond, toward Ala Moana. In Honolulu, one of the nation's fastest-growing cities, shopping at Ala Moana has replaced churchgoing, midday dinner, picnics, as a family occupation on Sundays. ("Here in Hawaii we find that Sunday is the biggest shopping day of all," explains Henry Walker, Jr., cheerful president of Amfac, the fastest growing of Hawaii's Big Five firms. "It has to do with the deterioration of the American family as an institution, of course, but it's damn good for our business boom. The further away you are from New York the less you feel the impact of a recession. My, the East Coast gets excited so easily about recession, they're so provincial, so insular over there . . .")

An SDS rally two miles east of Ala Moana, at the University of Hawaii: The cream-and-rose-hued campus is heavy with breadfruit and avocados, resplendent with the crimson vulvas of the African tulip trees, the scarlet claws of the Indian coral tree, the purple petals of the jacarandas. It is high noon. Before the microphone stand a bevy of beautiful Nisei girls—second-generation Japanese—wearing orchids in their sumptuous waist-length hair, sleek as a black forest pool. "Rotcee is a no-no!" the girls chant, waving their black manes. Their voices waft soothingly across the somnolent campus. Some fifty students lie stretched out on the grass, interspersed with a few radical professors who talk of taking out Tahitian passports if things get bad in Hawaii. On the wall of a nearby building is tacked up a small pink poster which says: "Please DON'T visit Hawaii. Don't buy Instant Imitation Aloha in Heavy Syrup Distributed by Friendly Skies Air Pollution Corporation."

The rally is being held to protest the firing of the Reverend Larry Jones, a faculty member ousted the preceding spring for taking part in a demonstration against ROTC. The Reverend takes his place at the microphone. He is a bearded, six-foot-four California cleric who looks like Charlton Heston about to play the role of a surfing Christ. He wears white wide-wale corduroys chopped off high above his athletic thighs, and a huge peace emblem. The Reverend speaks his conscience in protesting the Vietnam war. There are some twenty-two thousand students at the University of Hawaii's Honolulu campus, one out of seven from the mainland. Fifty of them are attending the rally, half asleep on the grass. "Rotcee is a no-no," the lovely Nisei chant, their hair as lustrous as a mandarin's silk cape.

"It's like the nineteen fifties here," a mainland professor mutters. "It's like the Eisenhower days. Docility, docility. No hands raised in the classroom, not a question raised. All those Japanese students cramming for the top grades—and the rest, you can't get them off the beach."

The progressive professor is in Honolulu for his health, and is perplexed. He expresses a commonly heard complaint: "Polynesian paralysis." The Pacific, he says, is like an amniotic fluid that lulls all thought and wit out of a man's system. Living in Hawaii, he quips, is like living with a beautiful pubescent whore, alternating carnal satisfaction with bouts of terminal boredom. There is a growing resentment toward the *haoles,* the white mainland foreigners, he notes, but perhaps only the *haoles* can get a radical movement off the ground in Hawaii. How are you going to get the students protesting when they're out at the beach all the time?

• • •

"Do you know what *I* like best about Hawaii?" says Dr. Thomas Hamilton, who has served successively as president of the University of Hawaii and director of the Hawaii Visitors Bureau. "I'll tell you what I like best about Hawaii." He is a kind-faced man, whose office is in a Waikiki sky-scraper flanked by surfboard-rental stands and souvenir shops selling plastic figurines of the old Hawaiian gods. "The *nicest* thing about Hawaii is that when we select a beauty queen at the university we don't have just *one* beauty queen. We have a Polynesian beauty queen, a Chinese beauty queen, a Japanese beauty queen, a Filipino beauty queen, a Portuguese beauty queen, a Puerto Rican beauty queen, a Negro beauty queen, *and* a Caucasian beauty queen. Six, eight beauty queens all in a row. *That's* what I like best about Hawaii."

Straight out of Dr. Hamilton's window there is a splendid view of several hotels, set on Waikiki Beach frontage which is worth six million dollars an acre. Waikiki Beach is a surprisingly short and shallow strip of grayish sand teeming with bodies—Coney Island on an August Sunday. To the left of Dr. Hamilton's office window is the Duke Kahanamoku night club, where the state's singing star Don Ho bellows out "This Is America" to busloads of tourists digesting their first Hawaiian dinner of *poi* and baked pig. A few blocks away is one of the wonders of the fiftieth state, the Hilton Hawaiian Village Hotel, whose night club at one time boasted an Icecapades show in an indoor rink. In front of some hotels large, sad-eyed Hawaiians stand as bellhops and doormen, dressed in red loincloths.

"The ethnic mix here is the richest in the world," Dr. Hamilton continues, "so varied, so interesting to analyze. The Orientals, of course, are the wonder of the island. Look at the Japanese, one-third of the population, yet they control over half of the legislature. The Hawaiians, on the other hand, are the big problem, still at the bottom of the economic ladder, dropping out of school all the time, lots of them on welfare, don't seem to care about getting ahead in the world . . . And yet the Hawaiian is a very bright, industrious fellow."

"A very bright, industrious fellow," Dr. Hamilton repeats sadly, his eyes quizzical.

"If you want to know why we Hawaiians are at the bottom of the ladder just take a look at this school," Melissa says. She is a seventeen-year-old part-Chinese, part-Hawaiian student at Kamehameha School, which was founded in the 1880's for the exclusive education of children with Hawaiian blood. Kamehameha—Kam for short—is funded by the revenues of the Bishop Estate, which owns one-tenth of the land in the state. Its large, drab, barracklike buildings tumble down the side of a steep hill on the northern fringe of Honolulu. "About, face!" shouts the leader of a platoon of fourteen-year-olds in military uniform. ROTC training and the wearing of military uniforms have been compulsory at Kamehameha since 1916.

"There are three thousand students in this school," Melissa says, "which is supposed to preserve the Hawaiian culture. Whatever that's supposed to mean. Ever since Kam was founded, students have been forbidden to speak Hawaiian or even pidgin. Kam hasn't had more than four trustees with Hawaiian blood in its eighty-year history. Until recently they didn't even allow us to dance the hula. Yes, there is an ethnic-studies program in Hawaiian language and culture, but it's so little encouraged that there are about fifty kids enrolled in it. It's not only the fault of the school but also of our parents. Hawaiians of my parents' generation are confused. They want us to do well in the *haole*—the white— culture yet they don't want us to become haolefied. The *haole* trustees who run this supposedly Hawaiian school are confused too. They want to haolefy us enough to make us docile, without haolefying us enough to compete with them. What kind of jobs do Kam students look forward to when they get out of here? Fireman, police chief, bartender. All the income from one-tenth of the state's land goes into the funding of one lousy school that trains policemen. It's the greatest joke around. The *haoles* needed a service class of maintenance men and they've gotten it by making a school for the brightest Hawaiians of each generation and then breaking their spirit, breaking their Hawaiian identity. It's tough being a good student at Kam. When I make a good grade the kids say, 'No make A,' 'No make Ass'—that's pidgin for don't make a fool of yourself. But it also means Don't make the A grade, don't stand out in your peer group by achieving or you'll become isolated, nobody will talk to you."

She was a graceful, angry girl who also found herself isolated in her anger at the Vietnam war and the military.

"At Cambodia and Kent State time I was suspended for three days for wearing a black armband to class and going to a Moratorium at the university. About a dozen of us—all girls —went and got suspended. The boys are apathetic, they've had this military crap beat into them by the *haoles* since they're babies to make them docile. Four straight years of compulsory ROTC, uniforms four days a week. After Moratorium I was thinking of all kinds of plans to bomb buildings. Not necessarily the draft boards, but the buildings that symbolize what the *haoles* have done to the Hawaiians; I would have chosen the Dillingham Building, or the Bishop Estate Building. I was going to do it all by myself, I didn't know anybody who would join me. Then I calmed down, I guess there was a big fantasy element to it, you feel so isolated here as a radical."

From the Kamehameha campus there is the most sublime view available of Pearl Harbor and of the Tripler Army Hospital. Five miles northwest of it is Camp Smith, center of the U.S. Pacific High Command, the largest single military command in the world, its area of responsibility including two-fifths of the earth's surface. The defense industry is the principal item in the state's economy: one out of seven residents in the state is an American military man or his dependent. No state in the Union, Melissa notes, is more dependent on the Cold War than Hawaii.

"Secession!" Melissa says, clenching her fist. "That's the grooviest movement around. It's the only way to get rid of the military."

• • •

In the office of Honolulu's mayor, smiling Nisei girls in floor-length swaths of flowered cloth glide across a décor of the Neapolitan Mafia style: imitation Louis XV chairs upholstered in pale-gold brocade; tasseled drapes; scarlet-hued, deep-pile rugs. Mayor Fasi is an Italian boy from Hartford, Connecticut, who came to Hawaii as a marine in World War II and loved it so much that he took the first civilian ship back to Hawaii after the war. "You can't beat us for paradise," says Mayor Fasi, a cheery man with a pomaded pompadour. "Even if you're poor and hungry in Hawaii you can still go to the beach. And we don't have any of those racial tensions you've got on the mainland. Why, the way I was brought up, back in Connecticut, I was taught that the only good Jap is a dead Jap. And now look at me! I'm married to one."

Shreds of table talk:

A visiting professor to a wealthy retired American during lunch at her oceanside villa in Kahala, Honolulu's Beverly Hills: "It's quite extraordinary, Mrs. H., but I don't see any black people walking around Honolulu." The hostess: "Yes! Isn't it marvelous! There are so few! I was just saying to one of our politicians the other day, 'Let's continue to keep them out by keeping the plane fares high, and raising the hotel room rates.'"

An executive of a real estate trust which is the seventh largest landowner in the state: "The Japanese are everywhere. They haven't only taken over Hawaii. They're taking over in Africa, Australia, South America, they're even creeping into Europe, controlling oil fields here, factories there. If this goes on, the twenty-first century will be the century of the Japanese takeover. Mind you, I like to work with the Japanese. Give me a Japanese over a Chinese anytime, he's honest as the day is long. But there's a difference between getting along with a Japanese at the office and having him move in next door to you, a big difference."

A director of one of the Big Five firms, sitting on the top floor of a skyscraper in the Financial Plaza of the Pacific: "1954, that's the year the Oriental began to feel his oats in Hawaii. You had them coming out of your ears, all those Japanese going through college and law school on the G.I. Bill and then taking over the legislature. It got kind of tiresome, that monkey legislature."

A Hawaiian bus driver: "The Chinese stick too much to themselves. Our Filipinos are no good, get drunk all the time. Our Puerto Ricans are rough, lazy, no good."

A Caucasian professor, formerly active with Hawaii's Communist party: "I have anti-Hawaiian prejudices because of their lack of realism. They've blamed their woes on everybody else and never faced up to the failure of their own chiefs. They're stuck in the politics of nostalgia. The only thing they do well is fornicate and drink."

The scion of a part-Caucasian, part-Hawaiian chiefly family, walking toward the lawn tennis court, which an aging Filipino in coolie hat is sweeping for the afternoon game: "I carry this around to take care of those mainland hippies," he says, pointing to his large black cane. "I just don't understand those mainlanders any more who're coming in to ruin our islands."

Kalani: "Kill a Haole Day, that's the most satisfying thing around. That's when our high school gangs go out and beat up some military men."

"When's Kill a Haole Day, Kalani?"

"Christmas, Sunday, tomorrow, anytime."

During the past four years over half a million G.I.'s have walked into a mint-green clapboard building on the edge of Waikiki—florid with plastic leis and colored posters of Honolulu hotels—to begin their R and R, Rest and Recuperation, from the Vietnam war. The green barracks at Fort De Russy, where the soldiers are driven to after getting off the plane at Honolulu airport, is filled every hour of the day with scores of women who have come to Hawaii to spend five days with their husbands or sweethearts. One is struck by the variety of the women's attire and disarray. Some are self-assured and resplendently whorish in platinum cornucopia wigs and satin pants suits, others demure and nervous in girlish ginghams, others listless in jeans and curlers. They finger brightly colored booklets advertising wedding-ring shops, motorcycle and scuba-diving-equipment rental centers, hotels in which they can "live like a general and spend like a private." The official purposes of the R and R program are coolly set forth by the military in other pamphlets scattered over the coffee tables of the waiting room: "(1) Respite from rigors of tour, (2) Deters the inflation of the Republic of

Vietnam economy, (3) Bolsters economy of R and R site location."

In Fort De Russy's waiting room, there are hot-dog stands, a soda-pop machine, a Hertz car-rental booth, leis marked down to one dollar for the military, and two army chaplains to handle any emotional problems that may arise among the 5,000 G.I.'s a month who come from Vietnam for their R and R, providing Hawaii in good years with more than one-fifth of its tourist business. One chaplain is a Southern Methodist, graduate of North Carolina's Citadel College; the other is a Lutheran from Texas. Any ordained minister, they say, can become an army chaplain by taking a nine-week course in chaplaincy at Fort Hamilton, Brooklyn, at the foot of the Verrazano Bridge.

"What do you learn in your chaplaincy course, Reverend?"

"Oh, mostly to read maps and not make fools of ourselves in the military."

"Anything else?"

"Well, we're taught to handle all those kids parroting the anti-Establishment line. We get to learn how to turn them around. We learn to say to them, 'It's not killing that is good, it's defending your country that is good.'"

"Do you like the military chaplaincy, Reverend?"

"It sure is rewarding. It's not that I love the Army, but I just adore soldiers. I've just finished a six-month tour with the Green Berets. You should see how they beam at you when they get out of the helicopter, those boys so hungry for the Gospel!"

"How long does the soldier have on his R and R?"

"Five days, six nights. There's been some thought of extending it, but that would be bad, they might get used to their girls again."

"Any special problems you encounter, Reverend?"

"Well, last year we'd average one guy a week who refused to take the plane back to Saigon. He was usually a guy who'd seen a buddy killed. We'd take him to the psychiatric ward at the military hospital and in three days he'd be just fine, ready to get back on that plane to Vietnam."

"Any other problems?"

"Well, we're overworked, you know, there are just two of us to take care of thousands of G.I.'s a month. We have to handle several adultery problems a week. We have to handle forty marriages a week. . . Also, the G.I.'s are having more and more trouble recognizing their wives and sweethearts these days. Girls lose weight, gain weight, cut their hair, let their hair grow, change its color, buy a wig. They're so nervous they pass each other by, and it's our role to get them together."

The busload of G.I.'s is expected momentarily. The Lutheran chaplain starts pacing the room nervously like a performer about to go on stage. "Wait 'til you see him, he's sensational," says a pretty WAC official from R and R called Captain Lawless. "It took us three years to figure out what to do with these weeping nervous women who'd come all the way from the mainland to see their loved ones. Finally we realized that what we needed was a *fun* chaplain, someone who could make them laugh. This chaplain is so great that people come in from the streets just to watch him."

"Here's the Hertz car stand, girls," the chaplain begins, "where you and your guy can rent a car to see these gorgeous islands with. Here's the lei stand where we give you an orchid lei at a special discount . . . I said an *orchid* lei. Here's the food stand, noted because it serves the world's most beautiful girls and most nervous women. Now, this is not a time to diet, girls. I understand you're nervous; if you're not you'd better see your doctor or a chaplain . . . but if you've chosen this day to diet, the adrenaline is going to squirt into your body and you're going to go to the hotel and your guy will be carrying some booze and you'll say to him, 'Fix me a little drink, honey,' he'll fix you a double Scotch and you'll pass out right in bed. Now, you wouldn't want that, would you, girls?"

A round of nervous dormitory giggling. Squeals: "He's *fantastic.*"

"Now these guys have been snatched from the steaming jungles of Vietnam," the chaplain continues, "and they come in full of bugs and roaches and creepy crawly things smelling pretty *high* . . . but don't worry, we've scrubbed them up already back at the Honolulu airport and given them a shot of booze to calm down their nerves. Now, in case you're interested, the Protestant service is at eight-fifteen, the Catholic one is at eleven—that's because we Protestants like to beat the Catholics to the beach. Don't skip our briefing after your guy gets in because we'll give you a tag for a fifty percent discount on hotels, booze, muumuus . . . When I tell you the bus is arriving there will be no more smoking, gum chewing, smacking your lips or goosing each other while you're standing in line . . . the bus is just two minutes away . . . See those people in the back there? They're waiting for the show to start . . . so one hand on his shoulder, girls, the other hand on your dress so you don't expose too much under your mini skirts . . . Look gay, girls, we've brought these guys from the war for you . . . Here they come . . ."

The G.I.'s walk in, blank-faced, dazed, their eyes darting back and forth between the two lines of bent, expectant women. They find their women and lunge. Soon the room is filled with embracing, weeping couples, exchanging deep and immeasurably long kisses. By the Hertz counter a crowd of onlookers smirk at the R and R show. The fun chaplain wipes his brow and looks anxiously at his watch. There will be another planeload of G.I.'s arriving from Vietnam in an hour and a half.

Kalani and I are driving around Mount Tantalus, on whose steep slopes thrives one of the most luxuriant rain forests in Hawaii. At the bottom of the mountain are the lands of the Hawaiian Homes Commission where anyone with half-Hawaiian blood or more can get an acre of land if he has the patience to wait ten, fifteen, twenty years. Halfway up the mountain are the splendid homes of some of Honolulu's most fastidious millionaires. The top of the mountain is the hippies' favorite site for tripping. Driving toward the Hawaiian Homes Commission land, Kalani points to a clapboard house, flanked by obese breadfruit trees, on whose stoop sit two round-cheeked, nutbrown children.

"Here are our ghettos," Kalani says proudly. "Are they much worse than the ghettos on the mainland?"

"Oh, no, Kalani, they don't begin to be as bad."

He looks disappointed. "Then I don't want to go to the mainland," he says. "I'm enough of a flaming radical already."

He makes a growling sound. "We Hawaiians used to be a very violent people," he says, "and we can become violent again."

Kalani's gentle, luscious brown eyes try to glimmer fiercely in his big, kind face. Kalani is a leader of the new nationalist movement that is asking the big landowners to return land to the Hawaiian people, and demanding a cessation of tourism and inmigration from the mainland. Kalani never liked school and seldom read a book until 1970, when he read *The New Indians, Manchild in the Promised Land, The Autobiography of Malcolm X,* all of Rap Brown, all of Eldridge Cleaver, and every other book he could find on the Black Power and Brown Power movements. The Hawaiians, Kalani says, have taken the white man's bullshit long enough. The tourist industry has created an image of the docile, smiling, sleepy, ukulele-strumming Hawaiians, but soon, he warns, the *haoles* will learn that the Hawaiians are not so gentle.

We are halfway up Mount Tantalus, crossing into a rain forest heavy with tropical fern and shimmering rubber trees, redolent with jasmine, guavas, ginger. Kalani takes a long, appreciative whiff.

"Hey, smell that ginger," Kalani exclaims. "When I smell that ginger I become less of a flaming radical."

II

On a February day in 1779 Captain James Cook fell face down on a shelf of black lava at the edge of the cobalt-blue sea on the island of Hawaii, killed by a native's blow. His death had come during a skirmish when the Hawaiians stole a cutter from one of his ships. Trembling, pale-green branches of the feathery kiawe tree brush the black lava upon which fell the greatest explorer of the eighteenth century. The site of the incident, at the edge of Kealakekua Bay, is very beautiful and has changed little since Cook's death. It had been inconspicuously marked until 1874, when the British government was ceded the land by the Territory of Hawaii to build Cook a pompous white obelisk. Employees of the British consulate come every few years to repaint the solitary, rarely visited monument. To this day there is no road or footpath to approach this memorial to one of the few white men in history ever killed by a Hawaiian. One can travel to it only by boat.

On the face of the obelisk is engraved: "In memory of the great circumnavigator, Captain James Cook, R.N., who discovered these islands on the 18th of January in A.D. 1778, and fell near this spot on the 14th of February A.D. 1779."

In 1970 some bold graffiti in scarlet paint were added to the left face of the monument: "To the memory of the great

Hawaiians," the scribbling says, "who discovered Hawaii in the year 1200. All power to the people."

The date is wrong: Hawaii was probably settled by a migratory wave from the Marquesas Islands between the years 300 and 700, and by a second migration from the Society Islands around 1200. But no matter. Kalani Ohelo and other nationalists say that the Hawaiians have to become proud before they can become historical.

Captain James Cook was killed partly because he was taken for a god, and was expected to behave like one. There prevailed at the time of his arrival the bittersweet myth of the god of agriculture, Lono, whose character is typically Hawaiian in its combination of Hamlet and Samurai, of tenderness and violence. Lono, as the story goes, had killed his human wife, whom he suspected of infidelity. Later, when he realized that she had been innocent, he sailed away in grief, promising to return someday when he had purged his guilt. It was in Lono's honor that the Hawaiians every winter used to hold the great Makahiki festival, a weeks-long bacchanalia of feasting, tax gathering, artistic and athletic contests. During this yearly olympiad fighting was suspended, prisoners were freed, some rigid tabus of the Hawaiian religion were lifted, and the symbols of Lono—large wooden sticks hung with swaths of white *kapa* (bark cloth)—were carried around the islands. When James Cook first landed on the Hawaiian island of Kauai in 1778 on his way to search for a northwest passage to the Atlantic, he arrived at the time of the Makahiki festival; the sails of Cook's ship, the *Resolution*, seen from afar as pieces of white cloth fluttering on the wooden post that was his mast, strikingly resembled Lono's symbol. For reasons in part political, the priests of Lono, in a quest for increased power, pronounced Cook to be the god returned. The explorer was worshiped with all the ceremony and bearing of gifts appropriate to deities.

One thinks of another destroyer of a culture, Cortés, arriving in Mexico two hundred years earlier with the attributes of Quetzalcoatl. But the infinitely more benign Cook had the misfortune to be twice mistaken for a god. A year later, when he landed a second time in the Hawaiian islands —this time at Kealakekua Bay on the island of Hawaii—he again arrived at the time of the Makahiki festival. But this time the festival was drawing to a close and the enthusiasm of the natives for Lono was waning. It was on this occasion that the Hawaiians stole one of Cook's cutters; the explorer, giving in to one of his famous bursts of temper, fired his musket into the crowd in an attempt to recapture the boat. At the height of the squabble between his men and the Hawaiians, Cook was struck at the back of the neck and fell at the water's edge, and then was stabbed and clubbed to death. To be sure, the islanders took certain precautions in case he was a god. A few Hawaiians are said to have helped themselves to his potential *mana*, his sacred power, by eating his entrails. Some of Cook's flesh was scraped off his bones and given a decent godlike burial in a place of total secrecy, as Hawaiian custom requires for the burial of all great chiefs. Upon the urgent demands of Cook's crew, the Hawaiians sent a few of the explorer's bones back to his ship.

Probably standing at the scene of Cook's death, and he

may have given a few blows himself, was a shrewd young chief called Kamehameha. Some accounts have it that he kept Cook's hair, and that its *mana* was responsible for his extraordinary rise to power. For Kamehameha was an upstart, a chief who rose to absolute kingship within three decades of Cook's death by the barrels of white men's guns. He has been called the greatest political genius of the Polynesian people, the Napoleon of the Pacific. He was the only leader in that vast third of the planet's surface who ever managed to unite any chain of islands into one kingdom. The few portraits of Kamehameha executed during his lifetime show a powerful, squat face in which the shrewd eyes and the savagely flattened nose contrast strongly with the compassionate and anxious mouth. One thinks of his life as a nightmare of narrow options. The Polynesian Maoris of New Zealand chose to fight the white men unto death, and retained their land and a good part of their culture. The great Kamehameha chose the opposite course. It was part of his Hawaiian cunning and pacifism to welcome the white men, to use them as tools to attain absolute power over his rival chiefs; and the intruders, in return, took advantage of his calculated generosity to gain control of his islands. The Aloha spirit, from the start, has been the Hawaiian's way of tolerating rather than fighting strangers, his way of avoiding direct confrontation. By 1800, white men had become the chief advisers at Kamehameha's court. He kept them as pets, married them to women chiefs and gave them the choicest foods. Isaac Davis, a Welsh sailor, ruled for a decade as governor of Oahu and had several hundred Hawaiians in his employ. He was succeeded by Oliver Holmes, an American who was addressed as Chief. The Englishman John Young was governor of the island of Hawaii, where he lived in a complex of fine white stone houses. He was also the admiral of Kamehameha's fleet from 1802 until the king's death in 1819, by which time there were some sixty Caucasians living on the island of Oahu alone.

One must admire the high diplomacy of this savage prince, Kamehameha, whose people, until Cook's arrival, had lived for centuries without a single contact with strangers. He had broken the power of antagonistic chiefs by appointing white men as governors of his most strategic islands. He weakened them further by breaking their large domains into scattered holdings and granting the most troublesome chiefs choice lands next to his capital, where he could keep an eye on them. By the time of his death Kamehameha had total control over the eight major islands of the Hawaiian chain—Oahu, Kauai, Maui, Molokai, Hawaii, Lanai, Niihau and Kahoolawe. The founder of Hawaii's dynasty is the only monarch whose burial site remains unknown to this day. Thus shrouded in the honor and mystery of legend, he has been venerated until lately as a demigod, the islands' only hero, the only Hawaiian ever commemorated with a statue. But one may always count on graffiti to reveal the temper of changing times, the fluidity of legends. In a Honolulu Public Library copy of R. S. Kuykendall's classic and voluminous history, *The Hawaiian Kingdom*, a fine penciled hand has recently scratched out the title of the third chapter, "Kamehameha and the Founding of the

Kingdom"; it has substituted, "The Beginning of the End."
The man revered for a century and a half as a founding father
is seen by some of the new Hawaiian nationalists as the traitor
who had the first and crucial choice, and who chose to open
his islands to the Westerners.

Settled later than any other major Polynesian islands,
discovered by explorers later than any other Pacific civilization, Hawaii lies two thousand miles away from the nearest
other island group. It is the most isolated archipelago in the
world. Most quirks of its history flow from its isolation. Pre-
cisely because they had never been challenged by any foreign values, the concepts of *mana* and tabu which pervaded
all of Polynesian society existed in Hawaii in their most rigid
form. Because they were so rigid, it was there that their
abolition would leave the deepest scars on the natives'
psyche. There were *kapu* (tabu) people, places, times, objects. Any profanation of their sacredness—misdeeds as mi-
nor as being touched by the shadow of a royal person, or
dropping the royal spittoon upon the ground—was held to be
highly disturbing to the equilibrium of the society and pun-
ishable by death. The *kapu* system was particularly prejudi-
cial to women, who, although their *mana* was often higher
than that of the men, had no access to the temples where the
political decisions were made. They were looked upon as the
dark, contaminated half of humanity, and were even forbidden under penalty of death to eat with men or taste the
islands' choicest foods. The strength of the high chiefs' *mana*
was preserved by careful inbreeding between pure blood
lines, as in Egypt, and the most desirable marriage was that

between a brother and a sister of equally high rank. Offspring of such unions were so sacred that they did not walk in the daytime for fear that their shadows might harm a subject, or that they would make the ground *kapu* and barren. The fabled corpulence of Hawaiian chiefs was in part caused by the fact that they were carried by attendants from childhood on so that their feet would not make the ground *kapu*. So rigid was the etiquette created by the hierarchy of *mana* that even the great Kamehameha had to approach the highest-ranking of his wives on all fours, because she had more *mana* than he. Through the political implications of the theocratic *kapu* system, the Hawaiian chiefs, whose genealogy was carefully preserved in family chants which traced their descent from the gods, ruled with a divine right. They were adulated by their people as in few other civilizations. "The ants weep, birds sing, pebbles rattle, bivalves mutter indistinctly, birds wither, smoke lies low, the rainbow arches, thunder roars, lightning flashes, rain rains, rivers flow, the sea roughens, waves snap, the horned coral flows up upon the land, the mournful cry of spirits wails loud, burying grounds awake . . . these are the witnesses of a great chief." Thus an ancient Hawaiian poem describes the chiefs' overwhelming power over man and nature.

Yet Hawaiian society was less oppressive, in some aspects, than many of the Mediterranean civilizations that are the predecessors of our own. Hawaii's land, theoretically, belonged to the gods. The common people, the *makaainana*, were free to move from one chief's land to another and worked under conditions of feudal discipline but not of serfdom. The chiefs therefore had to observe a modicum of civility to keep the *makaainana* in their employ. Accumulation was unknown in this economy of subsistence, which was devoid of all outlet for trade. Social competition was based on ideals of largesse, hospitality and generosity which still prevail among Hawaiian people. Warfare was often more symbolic than real, a ritual, athletic jousting prefaced by gigantic spouts of poetry and genealogical recitation, by much intimidating gesturing and grimacing. And it could be abruptly ended by the appearance of a chief so sacred that all soldiers had to throw themselves onto the ground.

Such were the features of many societies of the Pacific. The major trait which differentiated the Hawaiian from other Pacific islanders was a passion for innovation which one could define as a high degree of intelligence, and which made him swiftly throw away his stone ax upon the sight of a white man's steel blade. The ferocious Maoris had showered the first European intruders with arrows from their shore; the quiescent Australian aborigines had evidenced no more curiosity in the first white men's ships than in some species of sea bird. But the inquisitive and ebullient Hawaiians greeted the first ships with a joy and excitement displayed by few other Pacific islanders. And it was their greed for Western technology, the tragic side of their aloha spirit, which destroyed the delicate balance of Hawaiian society. If the men on Cook's ship received two pigs and several loads of fish from the Hawaiians in exchange for one iron nail, one can imagine the extravagant abundance of crops and animals which the chiefs forced the commoners to produce from 1780 on. As a growing number of trading vessels anchored at the islands a noncompetitive economy of subsistence was transformed with brutal rapidity into a forced economy of trade. The sandalwood trade with China, which flourished in the first two decades of the nineteenth century, brought increasingly oppressive labor conditions at a time when the Hawaiian people were being decimated by the white man's diseases. Lacking immunity because of centuries of isolation, Hawaii's native population fell from an estimated three hundred thousand to half that number in the forty years between Cook's arrival and 1820. It was further depleted by the white man's alcohol, which would remain the islanders' curse.

The dissolution of Hawaiian religion, which occurred several months before any Christian missionaries arrived, had an equally momentous impact. In his beautiful chronicle of Hawaii, *Shoal of Time,* historian Gavan Daws notes that the rigidity of the *kapu* system, the cornerstone of Hawaiian culture and religion, had depended on the islands' continuing and total isolation. An inevitable skepticism about it had grown in the time between the arrival of Cook and Kamehameha's death. There was the example of all those powerful white men who not only survived but fared splendidly without heeding the *kapus.* Since the Hawaiian religion had discriminated so stringently against women in all matters of politics and behavior, it is not surprising that its destruction was brought about by women, in a genuine mood of women's liberation.

The leader of this revolt was an ambitious, astute 300-pound beauty who was the greatest surfer of her day and had been the favorite of Kamehameha's twenty-one queens. Her name was Kaahumanu. Six months after her husband's death she managed—with the aid of another of Kamehameha's widows, the mother of the new young king, Liholiho—to destroy the *kapu* system in one stroke. The two queens scheduled an enormous feast and invited the weak and dissolute new ruler to break one of the most sacred *kapus* by eating with the women. Liholiho acted as some future Hawaiian monarchs would act when faced with a serious decision: a few days before the scheduled feast he went to sea with a boatload of liquor to consider the issue. Returning to the women's quarters in time for the repast, he wavered a few moments, then lurched to the women's feast and ate voraciously. This violation triggered a considerable rampage. In the next months Kaahumanu's followers swept through the islands destroying the old temples and burning their ancestral idols, which included some of the most superb wood carvings in Polynesia and some of the world's most exquisite feather work. Thus Hawaii's religion was destroyed by its chiefly caste—a unique phenomenon, since the dissolution of religion typically starts at the bottom of primitive society and not at its apex.

The first companies of Protestant missionaries arrived from Boston several months after these events and took advantage of the process of destruction which the Hawaiian chiefs themselves had instigated. Kaahumanu ruled as regent of the Hawaiian kingdom until 1832, and further accelerated

the transformation of Hawaiian society by becoming the missionaries' most ardent supporter. The native religion continued to be observed by a minority of Hawaiians—mostly
commoners—and went underground. Whatever temple
idols remained were hidden and worshiped secretly. The
gods of fishing and planting continued to receive the first
fruits. Bones of dead chiefs were revered as before. Obei-
sance to the powerful goddess of volcanoes, Pele, continues
to this day, as does the old art of the *kahunas*, medicine men
and healers.

Diderot: "One day the Christians will come, with their
crucifix in one hand and their dagger in the other, to cut your
throats or force you to accept their customs and opinions."
It is unfortunate that the evangelizing of Hawaii should have
fallen to Calvinists, who are notoriously more apt to force
their customs on others than other Christian sects. And the
first company of missionaries to arrive in Hawaii, under the
leadership of the Reverend Hiram Bingham, were right-
wing Calvinists at that. They were men who had chosen to
leave New England because they opposed liberal reforms
being enacted in segments of the Congregational Church in
the first decades of the nineteenth century. That church had
suffered a split, in those years, between proponents of die-
hard predetermination and reformist, more liberal men who
believed in greater free will and tolerance. Bingham and his
colleagues were of the first conviction: ultra-Calvinists who
wished to leave New England to escape what they saw as a
heretically progressive trend.

Bingham's company traveled to the Pacific to preserve

their rigid theories of predestination intact. In Hawaii they confronted a society devoid of the sense of sin with the most sin-ridden view of man ever offered by a Christian faith. Even their choice of Hawaii had an element of preelection about it. In 1809 a Hawaiian orphan named Opukahaia, who had been harshly mistreated by his foster parents, had swum out into the same bay where Captain Cook, three decades earlier, had met his death. He climbed onto an American fur-trading ship and begged to be taken back to the white man's land. Opukahaia was strongly moved, on his way back to New England, by the rudiments of Christianity he learned from his fellow passengers. A few months later the ship landed in New Haven, and soon some Congregationalist ministers found the young Hawaiian sitting on the steps of Yale College, seeking further instruction in the faith. Opukahaia's accounts of island mores alarmed the reverends. Finding him uniquely gifted, they sent him to the Mission School in Cornwall, Connecticut, where he was trained to lead the first company of missionaries to his homeland. The man who prompted the Calvinist evangelization of Hawaii died a year before he was destined to sail back to his islands, and to this day lies buried in a quiet Connecticut valley.

Bingham and his companions were earnest, dedicated, tragicomic figures, whose search for sin was as passionate as J. Edgar Hoover's hunt for Communism. They saw it in every traditional detail of Hawaii's brilliant culture, in the recitation of native poetry and in the playing of Hawaiian games and music, in the art of native wood carving and in the most inoffensive hula dance. ("Just watch the hands," the terrified missionaries would whisper to their children when they were exposed to this great art of the Pacific. "Just watch the hands.") The first white clapboard houses which the missionaries built and in which they lived under most arduous conditions, often packed ten or twelve to a tiny room, still stand today in downtown Honolulu. It is a testament to their suffering, their selflessness, their dedication, and their comic intransigence. With the same doggedness with which they continued to wear long-sleeved New England woolens in a sweltering climate, and exhorted the natives to do likewise, they built low-ceilinged rooms to retain the heat of their Honolulu fireplaces; and to teach their tropical flock to read, they used alphabet books with pictures of children skating, sledding and chopping pine trees in a snowy New England landscape. Eighteenth-century explorers, whose adulation of the noble savage inspired great admiration but little concern for the Hawaiians, had unwittingly triggered the collapse of Hawaiian culture by the sheer force of historical encounter. The missionaries, who had no admiration for the islanders but that most dangerous of loving concerns which expresses itself in evangelism, completed the process of cultural genocide within a few decades by making Hawaiians ashamed of being Hawaiian. The Polynesians today are among the most dispossessed people of contemporary Hawaii. One must search for the source of their troubles in the profound schizophrenia instilled in them by the first missionary companies —the neutralization of their identity, a national death wish. This island people weakened by centuries of isolation lacked the psychological antibodies, as well as the physical ones, needed to survive such sudden contact with the white man.

It is said that the Hawaiian had an uncanny way of predicting his own death. "I shall die next Thursday," he would tell his relatives. And die on Thursday he did, without doing physical violence to himself or showing symptoms of any disease. Other Hawaiians chose suicide to heal the split in their soul, or died of sheer schizophrenia.

Emily Kuihelani was a Hawaiian of chiefly rank who as late as the 1880's still believed in her old family gods. For centuries the shark had been sacred to her ancestors, a creature to be tamed, frolicked with and revered. Her husband, the son of American missionaries, had surreptitiously gone shark-hunting for many years without her knowing about it. When she discovered him at this sport she prepared a cup of poisoned *kauwe*, the herb potion with which Hawaiians had traditionally ended their lives when dishonor came upon them, and took her life by the seashore in front of her grieving relatives.

The beautiful Princess Nahienaena, a sister of Kamehameha III and his favorite concubine, was torn between her passionate and very traditional love for her brother and the sense of guilt imposed upon her by her missionary teachers. Weeping and laughing in turn in the royal pews of the churches, alternating between bouts of debauchery and fits of the deepest Calvinist piety, she died in 1834 shortly after her brother's child was born to her. She still lies buried at Lahaina, on Maui, a few blocks away from the psychedelic bikini shops of a hotel-studded resort that has become the St. Tropez of Polynesia.

There is a sense of historical justice about the demise of the Congregationalists' mission in Hawaii. Their failure to reconstruct a New England town in the Pacific was extreme. In the next several decades Mormons would make powerful inroads into the islands, their mission aided by their legend that the Hawaiians were one of the lost tribes of Israel; the Church of England would sweep into power with the support of the monarchy; and notwithstanding the harassment they suffered in their first decades on the islands, the Roman Catholics would eventually become the largest single religious body in the islands. As Hawaii became the Pacific's main provisioning and trading post for the whale trade and the clipper commerce with China, Honolulu grew to be one of the liveliest and most dissolute complexes of grog shops and sailors' whorehouses in the world. By the mid-nineteenth century dancing and drinking abounded in all circles, including many missionary families. In the 1860's the Hawaiian monarchs would give a costume ball at which the queen arrived dressed as Cybele, hardly a popular figure in Calvinist circles. The word "missionary," in contemporary Hawaii, would become a disdainful, semicomic term applied to prim styles of cotton frocks, to the more dreary modes of copulation or of social gatherings.

III

The Hawaiians had always had a dim instinctual fear that the United States threatened their independence. And the Hawaiian monarchy, from its beginnings, was strongly Anglophile. In 1810 the great Kamehameha I had written a letter to George III in which he referred to himself as being "subject" to the British king. It is to England that his son Kamehameha II, the *kapu*-breaker Liholiho, had chosen to go in 1824 when he became the first Hawaiian chief to go to Europe. He traveled to London with his sister, who was also his favorite wife. Because of the islanders' fatal susceptibility to Western diseases, the royal youngsters swiftly died of measles.

But this tragedy by no means diminished the Hawaiians' preference for England. Few events created a greater revulsion against America in Hawaiian royal circles, some decades later, than the voyage abroad of Prince Alexander Liholiho, son of Kamehameha III. Having made his grand tour of Europe, the prince was asked, upon his arrival in the United States, to remove himself from a railroad carriage because of the color of his skin. The incident creates the only passionate entry in the prince's personal journal, which, though remarkably polished for his fifteen years, offers mostly bland accounts of consular receptions, fencing lessons and styles of dress. "The first time that I ever received such treatment—" the prince ruminates, "not in England or France or anywhere else. In this country I must be treated like a dog to go and come at an American's bidding. Here I must state that I am disappointed at the Americans. They have no manners, no politeness, not even common civilities to a Stranger. In England an African can pay his fare for the Cars, and he can sit alongside Queen Victoria. The Americans talk and think a great deal of their liberty, and strangers often find that too many liberties are taken of their comfort . . ." Anglophilia also prevails among the monarchy's accouterments still preserved in Honolulu's Bishop Museum and in the remains of their sad palaces. This Oceanic royalty attired in laces, black velvets and tiaras, sporting gold watches and Brittanic military decorations, mustachioed and coiffed according to the latest styles shown in *Punch*, throning in gilt Victorian chairs under the traditional feather emblems of Hawaiian chiefs, attempted a pathetic emulation of Balmoral under their tropical skies. But, although an overzealous British naval captain actually managed to annex Hawaii to Great Britain for five months in 1843, England was simply too far away from Hawaii to compete with the United States, which became solidly entrenched through the influence of the first missionaries, and of the New England-based whaling industry.

It is possible that the longest-lived of the Hawaiian kings, Kamehameha III, might have turned back the encroaching tide of American power if he had been of stronger character. But he was wracked by alcohol and by his lasting grief over the death of his mistress and sister Nahienaena. He frequently left the affairs of state to go to Lahaina and brood at her grave. He reigned for almost thirty years, until 1854, and it is during those decades that the increasingly large numbers of American merchants and missionaries settling in Hawaii came to power, writing into the Hawaiian constitution whatever laws might fit their interests. The first advisers to the king after the great Kamehameha's death were missionaries, but almost any American could burrow his way to power with amazing ease. John Ricord, a New York barrister, became Attorney General of the Kingdom within a fortnight of his arrival in Honolulu. Another New York lawyer, William Little Lee, who had traveled to the Pacific to cure his consumption, was named chief justice of the Hawaiian supreme court while still in his twenties. Herman Melville, sojourning in Honolulu in the 1840's, called this royal entourage "a junta of ignorant and designing Methodist elders in the council of a half civilized king ruling with absolute sway over a nation just poised between barbarism and civilization." And some of these elders had very un-Yankee pretensions. Gerrit P. Judd, who served successively over a period of twenty years as Minister of Foreign Affairs, of the Interior, and of Finance, wore gold crowns on his coat, rode about Honolulu in a brocaded and gilded coach, and announced his arrival with a seventeen-gun salute. The kingdom, at the suggestion of the king's advisers, adopted the Code of Etiquette of the Congress of Vienna to settle matters of precedence at its official receptions, at the first of which the British consul general had a fistfight with the American attorney general.

There are many bitter sayings about "the missionary

monarchy," as Hawaiians called the white power structure in Hawaii. "The missionaries told us to look up to heaven," so goes one of the bitterest, "and while we did so, they stole our land." Notwithstanding its reputation of luxurious abundance, Hawaii is a chain of precipitously steep, volcanic islands in which only 15 percent of the terrain is arable. Fertile land is precious and its scarcity has been a key factor in its history. No restructuring of Hawaiian society engineered by the Americans was more important than the division of land, or Great Mahele, which is responsible for the amazing centralization of real estate ownership that still prevails in contemporary Hawaii. As of now, some 80 percent of the privately owned acreage in the state belongs to twenty individuals or corporations. An equally significant statistic is that fourteen individuals or corporations control—through ownership or leasing—40 percent of all Hawaii land.

Under the terms of the Great Mahele of 1850, the king gave up his rights to much of his former property, keeping certain estates which became known as crown lands; 245 high chiefs received some 1.6 million acres, which, with unmatched insouciance, they proceeded to sell, lease or give away to foreigners; commoners, foreigners and natives alike, could buy lots in fee simple from the rest of the islands' acreage. Ostensibly designed to abolish Hawaii's ancient feudalism, the Mahele created a new feudalism under the white man. The result was a totally Western concept of property conceived to suit the Americans' growing entrepreneurial and agricultural ambitions in the islands, and Hawaii's foreign residents were quick to take advantage of the "reform."

One of Kamehameha's former ship pilots was awarded 2,500 choice acres near Diamond Head, and another old-time American resident was granted 7,000 acres. But for the Hawaiian to obtain his plot entailed endless bureaucratic registration—filing of claims in writing by certain deadlines—which he was not equipped to understand. Of some seventy-two thousand Hawaiians still alive in 1850—diseases had again reduced the population by half in the three decades since the missionaries' arrival—only about ten thousand received land. But it amounted to only some 28,000 acres, or less than one percent of the islands' total acreage of four million. The Hawaiians had become gypsies in their own country.

The stories of the chiefs' giveaways have become legendary. A Hawaiian schoolteacher still remembers her grandmother selling several hundred verdant acres near Honolulu for a jug of wine. Kamehameha IV sold the entire island of Niihau for ten thousand dollars to a Scotch family that had come to Hawaii via Australia, whose descendants, the Robinsons, still own it, strictly barring it to visitors to this day. The readiness of Hawaiian women of chiefly rank to marry American men—pale skin had always been admired throughout Polynesia, and there had been a great cachet in bearing a half-Caucasian child—further enabled Americans to build up enormous estates.

The most tragic misuse of island land, in the eyes of many modern Hawaiians, was that of the Bishop Estate, the crown lands inherited by the last descendant of the Kamehamehas, Princess Bernice Pauahi Bishop. These lands comprised over 10 percent of the islands' acreage, and according to her last will and testament their entire revenues were meant to be used to support a school for children of Hawaiian blood. Because of her early death in 1884 and her American husband's close associations with Hawaii's white elite, the Kamehameha School became in reality a *haole* enterprise to keep the Hawaiian subjugated and docile. Boys were taught the trades that would make them good mechanics, carpenters and maintenance men; speaking Hawaiian was forbidden; and college enrollment has been insignificant in the eighty-five years of the school's existence. Until a few years ago Kamehameha girls were taught, in their home economics classes, to set tables with three sizes of wine glasses and four settings of silver knives and forks, "because it was evident," as a contemporary student put it, "that they needed us as maids."

The incentive for large landholding increased with the rise of Hawaii's sugar economy, which, unlike other crops, cannot be developed where a small, independent freeholding system prevails. The provisions of the Great Mahele enabled sugar planters to collect vast tracts of land from the government or from the chiefs. Cane had always grown wild in Hawaii. It began to be vigorously exploited in the 1860's after the demise of the whaling trade, which had been the basis of Hawaii's economy and which came to an end with the Civil War. The Civil War had also disrupted the sugar plantations of the American South, allowing Hawaiian sugar to enter the American mainland in large quantities. It was the decision of Hawaii's American oligarchy to create a one-crop economy in the islands. By the 1890's King Sugar, as the crop was called, would rule four-fifths of Hawaii's arable land under the control of a few score of powerful Americans. They were an efficient and hard-headed group, whose philosophy was succinctly expressed by missionary descendant Sanford B. Dole, the leader of the American elite that would over-throw the monarchy and engineer Hawaii's annexation to the United States. "I cannot help feeling that the chief end of this meeting," Dole stated at a planters' convention in the 1880's, "is plantation profits, and the prosperity of the coun-try, the demands of society, the future of the Hawaiian race only comes secondarily if at all."

Accompanying the rise of the sugar planters' power was the growth of increased nationalism and anti-Americanism among Hawaii's royalty, chiefs and commoners. Hawaiian nationalism became a political reality during the reigns of Hawaii's last two monarchs, King Kalakaua and Queen Lili-uokalani, two strong-willed persons who might have pre-served the identity and the pride of the Hawaiian people had they ruled fifty years earlier. David Kalakaua, the most intel-ligent and determined ruler to come to the throne since the great Kamehameha I, was a man profoundly devoted to Ha-waiian culture. He collected and stored the stripped bones and magnificent feather cloaks of ancient Hawaiian chiefs, and laid the foundation for the study of Hawaiian archeology. He commissioned the first transcription of the *Kumulipo*, the beautiful creation chant that is a basic text of Hawaiian mythology. He sponsored great festivals of Hawaiian singing and dancing and created a secret society restricted to men of Hawaiian blood, the Hale Naua, one of whose objects was "the revival of the ancient sciences of Hawaii." He was a gifted writer and musician, and his best-known poem is still heard today in the words of "Hawaii Ponoi," the islands' anthem.

Kalakaua, however, was a spendthrift, and suffered from delusions of grandeur. His attempt to make Hawaii the center of a great confederation of Polynesian islands, for which purpose he sent ambassadors throughout the Pacific, was a visionary but comic failure. He built himself a large, sad palace on King Street, and allowed the national debt to climb from $380,000 to two and half million dollars in a decade. Kalakaua had begun by pleasing the Americans, particularly through his support of the Reciprocity Treaty, which would later give the United States control of Pearl Harbor in exchange for duty-free access of Hawaiian sugar into the United States. But his reign ended in scandal, partly through his high living and his increasing efforts to revive Hawaiian culture, partly through several political blunders, the major one of which was his sponsorship of Claus Spreckels, an independent California-German sugar magnate detested by the Hawaiian planters. In 1887 a so-called Hawaiian League, representing the interests of the older-established planters, merchants and other Americans, and led by Lorrin A. Thurston, descendant of one of the first missionary families, broke the king's will under threat of arms. Their Bayonet Constitution restricted his power severely, abolished most of his favorite programs, and purged most of his political appointees. Kalakaua died in California, the last of the Hawaiian kings, leaving the throne to his sister, Liliuokalani, who was even more brash and militant a nationalist than he had been.

Queen Liliuokalani, who would make the last desperate bid for her islands' independence in the 1890's, was a fervent patriot whose stubbornness and integrity overshadowed her intelligence. In these days of renewed Hawaiian nationalism one sees an increasing number of photographs of her: an imposing, pug-faced woman with earnest, gentle eyes and a stubborn chin, dressed in emulation of the British Victorian court. Like her brother, she had a great gift for music. She wrote some of the most beautiful melodies still heard in Hawaii today, including the nostalgic, lilting farewell song "Aloha Oe." She was a conscientious Christian, and in her later years turned increasingly to the Church of England for solace, as had many Hawaiian chiefs.

Liliuokalani came to power the same year that an important Act of the U.S. Congress created a dire economic crisis in the islands and led its white elite to agitate seriously for Hawaii's annexation to the United States. The McKinley Act of 1891 removed duties on all imported sugar but also granted a bounty on sugar home-grown in the United States, thus destroying Hawaii's advantage under the reciprocity treaty. The planters clearly saw that Hawaiian sugar no longer had a protected market, and that the only way to keep themselves in the black was to have Hawaii annexed in order to benefit from the new laws that offered bounties on American sugar.

Although Hawaii's white elite, its planters and merchants, already owned or controlled four-fifths of the islands' usable land, they had only a few thousand votes under the prevailing constitution. And since the sentiments of the Hawaiian people were overwhelmingly against annexation, the planters prepared themselves for the eventual necessity of a military coup. They formed an Annexation Club, which would later change its name to the Committee of Safety (it was said that the planters were thinking back to the Jacobin Committee of Public Safety that ruled during the bloodiest years of the French Revolution). Their plans were accelerated by the news that Liliuokalani was secretly preparing a new constitution which would restrict the vote to true Polynesian Hawaiians. In January 1893, before the Queen was able to legalize her constitution, the Committee of Safety overthrew Liliuokalani with the support of the United States minister and four boatloads of American marines, but with none whatsoever from the American government in Washington. In that era of slow communications it took a good week to get news from Washington to Hawaii, and there were often large discrepancies between the views of the federal government and its Hawaiian ministry. The White House's stand on the Hawaiian issue remained all the more uncertain throughout this high-handed coup d'état because of a Presidential transition. In 1892 President Benjamin Harrison, reflecting the growing imperialism of the Republican party, had assured the annexationists that they had his support. He had sent the draft of an annexation treaty to the Senate which his successor, Democrat Grover Cleveland, withdrew early in the following year. Cleveland went further and stated that Liliuokalani had been illegally over-

thrown by an ill-advised American minister and unauthor-
ized marines, and that she should have her throne back
again. Congress strongly supported him. Voting on a resolution on the Hawaiian issue, the House of Representatives
overwhelmingly endorsed the principle of noninterference,
and declared the annexation of the islands "uncalled for and
inexpedient." But Hawaii's provisional government, the
"Missionary Monarchy," did not recognize the power of
President Cleveland to settle its domestic affairs, and declared Hawaii an independent republic in 1894. Washington
chose to avoid a confrontation and did not enforce its decisions. And so the planters' revolution, as bloodless as it was
both farcical and tragic, led by a few hundred Americans
protecting their landed wealth, remained incomplete for five
years. Larger events of American history, and the return of
a Republican administration under McKinley, would complete it.

The Hawaiians were as inexperienced at revolution as
the United States, in the nineteenth century, was inexperienced at annexing an overseas territory. Over the next
two years, Liliuokalani's royalist supporters went underground and armed themselves for insurrection with tropical
ineptitude. Bombs—some of them made with coconut shells
—were hidden in places as obvious as Liliuokalani's flower
garden and Waikiki Beach. In January 1895, following a confused plan of attack, the royalists started their rebellion
twenty-four hours ahead of schedule and were flushed out of
the bush in ten days. One of the largest ammunition dumps
was found in the Queen's flowerbeds. She was taken to court

alongside the leaders of her royalist troops, and sentenced to five years of house arrest. But she was paroled within the year. Even Hawaii's only revolution was suffused with gentle Aloha spirit. In a show of tolerance that would remain typical of Hawaiian politics, the five chief leaders of the royalist forces, who at first had been sentenced to death, were all freed within a year of the attempted coup. And the most revolutionary member of the five, Robert Wilcox, would be elected a few years later as Hawaii's territorial delegate to the United States Congress.

The acquisition of Hawaii had been engineered by the will of a handful of its American residents with singularly little long-range imperialist scheming on the part of the United States government. For until the 1880's, although insular expansionism had a few isolated proponents such as William H. Seward, it was highly unpopular. Some of the older Republicans were among its staunchest foes. They maintained that the framers of the Constitution had not contemplated noncontiguous territorial addition to the Union or the creation of an overseas colonial system. They argued that a territory like the Hawaiian Islands would be a source of military weakness rather than of strength. In both the debates over annexation and statehood, there would also be racist objections, on the part of Congress's more conservative members, against incorporating Hawaii's large nonwhite majority into the Union. "How can we endure our shame when a Chinese senator from Hawaii"—these were the words of Congressman Champ Clark in 1898—"with his pigtail hanging down his back, with his pagan joss in his hand, shall rise from his curule chair and in pigeon English proceed to chop logic with George Frisbie Hoar or Henry Cabot Lodge? *O tempora, O mores!*"

However, the doctrine of insular expansion began to acquire champions in the late 1880's and 1890's, when the American economy sank into a depression theretofore unparalleled in its history. By that decade the era of arable, free public land had ended. United States warehouses were glutted and prices declined sharply. Republicans in particular began to look upon overseas expansion as a restorative. They saw Pacific islands, such as Hawaii, as way stations for exporting surpluses to the boundless markets of China. The growing interest in Hawaii's annexation was also strongly linked to the rise of navalism, whose leading exponent was the naval officer Alfred T. Mahan. Mahan's article "Hawaii and Our Future Sea Power," published in 1893, had great influence. Reasoning that the future growth of the United States was possible only at sea, he argued that Hawaii could serve the United States' interests as the Gibraltar of the Pacific. It was under the inspiration of Mahan that leading proponents of the new imperialism, such as Henry Cabot Lodge, began to argue that control of Cuba, of the forthcoming Isthmian Canal and of Hawaii complemented each other in a logical pattern of growth.

Hawaii's fate was finally sealed by the outburst of imperialist sentiment brought about by the Spanish American war. Shortly after the Battle of Manila, on June 15, 1898, a resolution to annex the Hawaiian Islands was brought before the House. This time, adoption was passed by 209 yeas (of which

178 were Republican, 22 Democratic) and 91 nays (5 Republican, 78 Democratic). The Senate acceded with equal readiness. And on July 7 President McKinley signed the resolution into law. At the ceremony of annexation the Hawaiian anthem written by King Kalakaua, "Hawaii Ponoi," was played for the last time as the official anthem of the islands, and the Hawaiian flag was hauled down. "As the last strains of Hawaii Ponoi trembled out of hearing," an emotional observer wrote, "the wind suddenly held itself back. The Hawaiian flag . . . dropped and folded, and descended lifeless. The American flag climbed slowly on its halyards and . . . the trade wind breaking from its airy leash, caught it in its arms, and rolled it out to its full measure."

After annexation there was one more chance, and an excellent chance at that, for the Hawaiians to find self-determination in their government. But they bungled it again through the weakness and self-indulgence of their chiefs. When political parties began to organize for the first territorial election, the Hawaiians did not support the established mainland parties—Republican and Democratic—jousting for the first time on the islands. Instead they gave their votes to a third group which campaigned under the name of the Home Rule party. Their leading spokesman was Robert Wilcox, the part-Hawaiian head of Liliuokalani's forces. The slogan of the Home Rulers, who insisted on speaking Hawaiian in Congress, was *Nana i ka ili*, "Look at the skin." The Home Rulers swept the first election of 1901, winning nine of the territorial Senate's thirteen seats and fourteen of the House's eighteen seats, and sent Wilcox to Washington as Hawaii's territorial delegate.

It was evident that the islands' American oligarchy would try to put an end to the Home Rulers' control. To regain electoral control of the islands, the Republican oligarchy sought a popular chief whom they could control. They found it in the person of Prince Jonah Kuhio Kalanianaole, a *bon vivant* and favorite of Liliuokalani's who, like Wilcox, had served a prison term in the uprising of 1895. They simply asked him to become a Republican, and to run against Home Ruler Wilcox. Kuhio, like most Hawaiian aristocrats, was a convivial card player and drinker who was greatly impressed with the glamour of Washington diplomatic life. A gentle, indolent man, whose nickname was Prince Cupid, Kuhio, like all Hawaiians of chiefly lineage, had enormous nostalgic appeal for his people. He was able to draw enough votes away from Wilcox's Home Rulers to be elected delegate to Congress in 1902, and nine more times after that. The Home Rule party died out in 1912. Kuhio served the Republicans so well that they remained in total control of the territory for four decades; they were so firmly entrenched that Democrats, until after World War II, would hold their organizational meetings in the most furtive of conditions—sometimes at midnight in moonlit swamps—to avoid being blacklisted by the Republican oligarchy.

IV

The spiritual destiny of Hawaii has been shaped by a Calvinist theory of paternalism enacted by the descendants of the missionaries who had carried it there: a will to do good for unfortunates regardless of what the unfortunates thought about it. Economically, it was shaped by the profit motives of a society of sugar planters whose regard for human autonomy was as narrow as that of the missionaries.

Between 1850 and 1930, some four hundred thousand men, women and children were transported to the Hawaiian Islands as a result of the sugar planters' relentless search for cheap and docile laborers. It was evident, as sugar began its phenomenal growth on the islands (its production quadrupled between 1896 and 1931, when it reached some two million tons a year), that there would never be enough of the depleted Polynesian people to create an adequate labor force. And the diligence of the Polynesian Hawaiians, who had been described by Enlightenment explorers as one of the world's most industrious lot, seemed to have been broken by the suppression of their religion and their culture. Terming these Polynesians as easy-going and temperamentally ill-suited to the tedious and arduous work of the cane fields, the planters looked elsewhere. The philosophy of their search for labor would be succinctly phrased by a trustee of the Hawaiian Sugar Planters' Association who said that there was "little difference between the importation of foreign laborers and the importation of jute bags from India."

The ethnic breakdown of this importation of human produce was roughly as follows: 180,000 from Japan proper and Okinawa; 125,000 from the Tagalog, Visayan and Iloco provinces of the Philippines; 46,000 South Chinese; 17,500 Portuguese from the Azores and Madeira Islands; 8,000 Koreans; 6,000 Puerto Ricans; 8,000 Spaniards; 1,300 Germans and Galicians; 2,000 Russians; and many other groups in smaller numbers. Although plantation wages were higher in Hawaii than in most other places in the world, the treatment of the workers was in keeping with the importation of jute bags. Life on Hawaiian plantations was far less violent, physically, than plantation life in the pre-Civil War South, but often equal to it in its psychological violence. The Penal Contract labor system, which lasted until annexation, was in effect forced labor, enabling workers to escape the cane fields only through suicide or desertion. After annexation, which abolished the Penal Contract clauses, conditions of forced labor continued in practice, if illegally, on many plantations: workers who caused trouble were ordered to move their families out of the plantation houses overnight; fourteen or more men sometimes slept together in rooms fifteen by twenty feet; the black snake whip continued to be used by some *lunas*, or overseers, who were most often chosen from the Scotch or Portuguese immigrant stock; the fine for the simple misdemeanor of trespassing was a whole day's wages; managers could dock the workers' pay without reason; and there was

no channel, until the 1940's, when unions finally got a foot-
hold in Hawaii, to protest the fact that the working hours
were often dictated by the overseers' whims.

What was specifically unique to the Hawaiian planters'
way of obtaining maximum profits was their tactic of "divide
and conquer." They pitted diverse ethnic groups against
each other to deter any united front among the workers. The
policy had been spelled out in 1895, when a planter testifying
before a special commission on plantation unrest stated that
"strikes will continue as long as men combine . . . the only
measure that can be taken are those which will reduce their
opportunities for combination . . . this can be done by em-
ploying as many nationalities as possible on the plantation."
It was the conscious strategy of the planters, therefore, to
welcome the arrival of each new racial group not only as an
addition to the labor force, but also as a curb upon the potential rebelliousness of its predecessors. It was also their
strategy to encourage dissent among Hawaii's varied ethnic
groups by holding to a large differential of wage scales according to race: in 1902, the average daily income of a skilled
worker averaged $4.22 for the Caucasian; $1.80 for the Hawaiian; $1.69 for the Portuguese; $1.22 for the Chinese; and
$1.06 for the Japanese, who, until World War II, would re-
main the most suspect and repressed members of Hawaii's
working force.

The Chinese had been the first of the Oriental groups to
emigrate to the islands, many of them of their own free will
before the ascendance of the sugar plantations. Coming from
a culture which had been based for thousands of years on a

competitive commercial economy, they showed, from the start, a phenomenal talent for accumulating and exhibiting wealth. By the 1850's some thirty Chinese merchants were doing so well in Honolulu that they gave a grand ball for the king and queen, spending some four thousand dollars on food and decorations, practicing quadrilles by the hour so they could join in the dancing. The Chinese who were contracted later for the specific purpose of plantation work turned out to be too gifted for business to last long in the cane fields. When not satisfied with plantation life, they never protested, as the Japanese would. They tended to leave for town and amass a fortune by becoming restaurateurs, tailors, laundry-men or bakers. "Ching Chong Chinaman, sitting on a fence, try to make a dollar out of fifteen cents"—so went a popular ditty in Hawaii at the turn of the century.

The Chinese in Hawaii also merged with amazing speed into the racial melting pot created by the sugar planters. They were devoid of the nationalism of the Japanese, for the China they had left behind them was not yet a united nation, and their chief loyalty was to their clan or kinship group. The great majority of them arrived single and swiftly married Hawaiian women. The pidgin dialect of Hawaii, which later came to be used by all of the islands' ethnic groups, was first evolved by the Chinese as a way of communicating with their native wives and part-Hawaiian children.

Coming from a culture which had always revered educa-tion, the Chinese spent amazing amounts of their incomes on schooling, and by the 1930's Chinese professional and busi-nessmen had penetrated some choice residential areas of

Honolulu theretofore reserved for Caucasians, areas which would remain closed to the Japanese for another twenty years. By the 1950's the median annual income of Hawaii's Chinese surpassed that of the Caucasians, and continues to do so today. Among Hawaii's most prominent contemporary millionaires—all descendants of indentured Chinese plantation workers—are U.S. Senator Hiram Fong, who grew rich through a vast network of financial companies in the islands; real estate entrepreneur Chinn Ho, who regaled himself at a recent birthday party with a silver-trimmed golf cart delivered by helicopter to the lawn of the exclusive Makaha Inn; and banker Hung Wo Ching, president of the inter-island Aloha Airlines, who became, in the last decade, the first non-Caucasian senior member of the Bank of Hawaii, the first non-Caucasian trustee of the Bishop Estate, and the first non-Caucasian director of a Big Five firm.

By the 1880's, the amazing capacity of the Chinese laborers to prosper in the towns had created a dilemma for the sugar planters. They found a temporary solution by importing several thousand Portuguese, but distance made their transportation expensive. The Portuguese would never be available in desirable quantities, and their pride in being Caucasians within an Oriental work force made them difficult to manage. The planters' eyes inevitably turned to Japan. The bad seasons that hit southern Japan in the early eighteen-eighties, bringing widespread starvation to the peasants, were auspicious for the Hawaiian planters. In those years their recruiting agents flooded Japanese villages, praising Hawaii's endless summer and its abundant money, and some 100,000 Japanese laborers were brought to Hawaii in the next three decades.

The ascent to power of the Japanese in Hawaii was infinitely more difficult and stormy than that of the Chinese. They were considered subversive by the Caucasian elite, who deeply feared their allegiance to Japan and its imperial ancestors. Their assimilation into Hawaii's melting pot was extremely slow; for to marry a non-Japanese was considered a dishonor, as it is in some Japanese Hawaiian families to this day, and the unmarried workers tended to send for picture brides from their own country. The strong cultural nationalism of the Japanese created a vast network of Japanese-language schools and newspapers which were considered suspect and unpatriotic by the oligarchy. And their complex sense of honor led them to rebel as the Chinese never had against those plantation practices which they saw as insulting to their people. Between 1890 and 1900 more than thirty plantation disturbances caused by Japanese workers were reported in the Honolulu press. ("Little Brown Men Run Up Against the Real Thing at Olaa," so went a typical headline. Or: "Is Hawaii to be Ruled from Tokyo?") The Japanese organized the first major strike in the Territory of Hawaii—on the island of Oahu—in 1909. The retaliations were so ferocious that one of its organizers, now in his nineties, has spent the rest of his life on the island of Kauai without daring to return to Oahu for fear of his safety. And the planters' solution, from 1910 on, was to import tens of thousands of Filipino laborers to curb the rebelliousness of the Japanese.

Another major strike on the territory occurred in 1920—

this time in cooperation between Japanese and Filipino workers. After this strike, life on the plantations became unbearable for the more aggressive Japanese. They were increasingly regarded as unassimilable. A concerted effort was made to destroy the Japanese-language press and the remnants of their labor movement. Throughout the 1920's, mounting threats concerning the yellow peril were expressed by the Caucasian elite. "Never lose sight of the real issue," the *Honolulu Star Bulletin* editorialized after the 1920 strike. "Is Hawaii to remain American or become Japanese?" As long as Japanese agitators could control the plantation laborers, the *Bulletin* warned, they would be "completely the masters of Hawaii's destiny . . . the autocratic dictators of Hawaii's industrialism . . . as if the Mikado had the power to name our governor and direct our political destiny."

In the 1920's the Japanese began to migrate in great numbers to Hawaii's towns, as the Chinese had decades before, finding work as machinists, painters, carpenters, fishermen and shopkeepers. It was also during that decade that the Japanese began to realize that they might find their road to power through politics. By the 1930's, they had become the largest ethnic voting block in the territory: one out of four registered voters was of Japanese ancestry. While the deeply conservative Chinese accepted the social order as it existed and rarely criticized the power elite, the Japanese provided the avant-garde of union leadership and left-wing politics. In his excellent sociological study of the islands, *Hawaii Pono*, Lawrence Fuchs notes that until World War II the

Japanese issue had Hawaii's Caucasian oligarchy stranded between the devil and the deep blue sea: if they did not become thoroughly Americanized the islands might become an extension of Japan in the Pacific; if, on the other hand, their Americanization was complete, the Japanese might vote as a bloc and elect political officials of their own race, which would be insufferable.

There was ambivalence, too, in the hearts of the islands' Japanese. The *Issei*—the older generation born in Japan—tended to hold strongly to their native culture and traditions. The *Nisei* and *Sansei*—second and third generations—would choose to become super-Americans. The test of their loyalty came with World War II. The panic which caused the internment of *Nisei* on the mainland was simplified in Hawaii by the fact that there were simply too many Japanese to intern: their imprisonment would have disrupted Hawaii's economy. Only their intellectual leaders—several hundred schoolteachers, newspaper editors and Buddhist priests who comprised less than one percent of Hawaii's Japanese population—were sent to relocation camps on the mainland. It was to prove their patriotism that the Japanese of Hawaii joined the 100th Battalion, later known as the 442nd Regimental Combat Team, which became the most valorous and highly decorated American fighting unit in World War II. It also had the greatest casualty rate. Called the "Go for Broke" or the "Purple Heart Battalion," the 442nd had been reduced from 1,563 to 268 fighting men in the three months between their landing at Salerno, Italy, and the battle of Cassino. Thus it was the Japanese of Hawaii, for decades so deeply suspect in their adopted homeland, who led the parade of victorious American forces through Rome a year later because of their extraordinary bravery in battle.

The heroes of the 442nd took advantage of their G.I. Bill of Rights and disabled veterans' compensation to go on to college and to law school (preferably to Harvard). It is partly for this reason that they acquired their vast political power in Hawaii, where today they control more than half of the state legislature and the majority of the judgeships in Hawaii's supreme court. Few Japanese success stories are more characteristic than those of Senator Daniel Inouye and U.S. Representative Spark Matsunaga, both sons of plantation workers, both gravely wounded in the 442nd. Daniel Inouye, who lost his right arm at Anzio, was instrumental in the rise of Hawaii's Democratic party, which finally triumphed over the Republicans in the 1954 territorial elections. He became U.S. senator in 1962, and in 1968 gave the keynote address and the seconding speech for Hubert Humphrey at the Chicago convention. Spark Matsunaga, who acquired his nickname through his agility on the football field, was brought up on a plantation in direst poverty. He had sold homemade *tofu*, bean curd, from door to door from the time he was six years old to help his family survive. After serving in the 442nd and graduating from Harvard Law School, he became a relentless lobbyist for Hawaiian statehood, and served six years in the territorial legislature. A Democrat, he has been reelected to his seat in the United States House of Representatives four times since 1962, and is considered the most liberal member of the prestigious Rules Committee. His militantly progressive Hawaiian colleague in the U. S. House of Representatives, Patsy Mink, is also of pure Japanese descent.

In one of the more poignant moments of James Michener's book on Hawaii, an American tells one of his compatriots: "You don't have your islands. The Japanese have them. You don't have the money. The Chinese have that. You don't have the land. The Fort has that."

Of all the groups that have come to prominence in postwar Hawaii, it is the Japanese who are the most symbolic of the new Establishment, and who are the most resented as such by the Polynesian Hawaiians. The white man had been difficult enough to compete with, in the classroom or the marketplace, for a people so swiftly snatched away from an oral culture and a primitive subsistence economy. The Orientals, with their millenia of written culture and their decorous stress on schooling and commercial competitiveness, have completed the dispossession suffered by the Hawaiians since the days of Captain Cook. And in the past two decades much of the old resentment that the Polynesians had felt against the Caucasians has been subtly redirected toward the super-efficient Japanese educator, storekeeper, politician, civil servant. The Japanese, in Hawaii, is the *apparatchik* of the system. He is to the Polynesian child what the white schoolteacher is to the mainland's black child; he is to the Polynesian adult what the honky is to the mainland's black man. "Who flunk me out of school?" a Hawaiian recently complained. "A Japanese. Who refused me a job at the garage and the grocery store because he had just given it to his relative? A Japanese. I go to the unemployment office and who tells me to sit down, get up, write my name? A Japanese. Now I'm on welfare and who's my caseworker? A Japanese."

The Chinese of Hawaii are less resented, perhaps because their inclination to intermarry has created a vast population of extraordinarily beautiful half-Polynesian people. But the Chinese also serve to reinforce the pathetic self-depreciation which Polynesians practice among themselves. "The reason you're so smart," a Polynesian parent will say to a child who does well in school, "is because you have a Chinese grandfather."

Yet in the curious pecking order created by the sugar planters, there is always a lowlier caste for the lowly to pick on. The Filipinos, until recently more dispossessed than the Polynesians, were the most deprived victims of the planters' search for docile labor. Most of them had come alone, determined to return to their *barrios* after they had made the fortune promised them by the planters' agents. Nine out of ten of them remained single. And although the planters' paternalism extended itself to a systematic importation of prostitutes to the Filipinos' barracks, their bachelorhood made homosexuality and violence inevitable. They were considered boisterous, uncouth sex fiends by other islanders. Devoid of the high regard for education held by other Orientals, they have had the highest rate of illiteracy of any people in Hawaii, and also the highest rate of suicide. Until recently they remained the islands' most politically apathetic group; in the territorial election of 1934 about a hundred Filipinos registered out of a population of a hundred thousand. To this day they remain the bulk of the small plantation force left in Hawaii's sugar-cane fields. And one of the saddest sights of Honolulu's Chinatown is that of the old retired Filipino men crowded in welfare dormitories, talking nostalgically of the Filipino *barrios* which they never earned enough money to return to.

"There is a government in this territory," an attorney general of Hawaii once said, referring to the islands' fabled Big Five firms, "which is centralized to an extent unknown in the United States, and probably as centralized as it was in France under Louis XIV." The Big Five (Castle and Cooke, Alexander and Baldwin, Theo. H. Davies, C. Brewer and American Factors [Amfac], which began as the German firm H. Hackfeld) were companies which had begun as sugar factors, or agencies, to serve the plantations; they administered the shipment, distribution and sale of the crop. Felicitously isolated from the mainland's labor movement, these companies formed a cartel that totally controlled Hawaii's economic and political life until World War II. By 1930, they controlled 96 percent of the islands' sugar crop and every business associated with sugar, which meant virtually all of the sizable business in the islands: banking, insurance, utilities, transportation, wholesale and retail merchandising, both inter-island and mainland shipping. In 1932 they also gained control of the pineapple industry, which had been pioneered at the turn of the century by James Dole in dusty soil not suited to sugar cane, and which remained Hawaii's second most important crop prior to World War II.

74

An estimated one-third of the directors and officers of the sugar plantations and agencies controlled by Hawaii's Big Five were direct descendants of the islands' missionary families, or related to them by marriage. And since the missionary families tended to marry among themselves, the nepotism in Hawaii's capitalist circles was unparalleled in any other area of the United States. One single family was represented on eighteen of the forty corporations listed on the Honolulu Stock Exchange in 1928. Five other families had members on five or more boards of directors. Frank Atherton was a typical Big Five official. He was president of Castle and Cooke and of the Home Insurance Company; vice president of American Factors, the Hawaiian Trust Company, the Territorial Hotel Company and the Hawaiian Electric Company; director of the Bank of Hawaii, the Hawaiian Pineapple Company and the Inter-Island Steamship Company. Since Atherton's mother was a Cooke, he was a cousin and close cooperator of Clarence Cooke, the president of the Bank of Hawaii, and of Richard Cooke, chairman of the board of another Big Five firm, C. Brewer. As for Richard Cooke himself, he was co-president of the Hawaiian Electric Company, the Hawaiian Agricultural Company and five major plantations; he also held directorships in the Hawaiian Electric Company, the Bank of Hawaii, the Matson Navigation Company, American Factors and the Mutual Telephone Company.

The Big Five had their offices in stately, columned buildings of the Palm Beach Egyptian style, which stood within two blocks of each other and a few hundred yards away from the Honolulu shipping docks, which they totally controlled.

("They were so close to each other," recalls Harriet Bouslog, a great labor lawyer whose work did much to break the Big Five's power, "that you could spit on all five of them at the same time.")

Thus the territory was run by a tight network of some one hundred Caucasians, most of them descended from the men who had maneuvered the deposition of Hawaii's last kings. They had almost all attended the prestigious, missionary-founded, overwhelmingly Caucasian Punahou School. They were all Republican and predominantly Congregationalists. They all golfed and drank together at the exclusive Pacific Club, which was founded in 1851 and which remained totally closed to Orientals until 1968. And they rarely allowed any personal differences to interfere with their cooperative control of the islands' wealth. Much of their efforts, until World War II, were directed at keeping mainland business out of the islands. In 1941, for example, Sears Roebuck decided to build a store in Honolulu despite the monopoly on retail trade held since 1850 by Honolulu's one major department store, Liberty House, a subsidiary of Amfac. Within a few months after it had begun negotiations, Sears' directors received veiled threats from Amfac that the Matson Lines— which monopolized all shipping to and from Hawaii, and was totally controlled by the Big Five—would not ship Sears products if Sears went through with its building plans. Sears managed to get a store built by threatening to buy its own ships for the project, but it was obliged to work secretly during the real estate negotiations by hiring two anonymous agents to collect parcels, house lot by house lot, in suburban Honolulu.

The economic power of Hawaii's Republican elite depended on their astute political control over the three key points of the islands' political life: the territorial legislature, the territorial delegate to Congress and the territorial governor. The latter was appointed by the President for four-year terms and had vastly greater powers than any mainland governor. The Big Five had started off well at the turn of the century by Republicanizing the Hawaiians' vote through Prince Kuhio. And they continued to lobby so skillfully in the next four decades that five out of six governors and a substantial number of Hawaii's legislators were Republicans who had administrative or policy positions in the major sugar agencies. Even Walter Dillingham, the one island magnate who was not within the Big Five complex, and who had made his fortune dredging out Pearl Harbor, kept his own paid lobbyist in Washington. "Big Sixth" Dillingham, whose firm still monopolizes the dredging on the islands, is said to have entertained every President, Vice President, Secretary of State and key senator of the United States during the forty years prior to statehood.

But the most amazing feat of Hawaii's Big Five was to render the Democratic party virtually impotent for the first four decades of the century. Some of their tactics were unabashedly illegal and high-handed. Many plantation managers hung pencils from the ceilings of voting booths so that they could tell from the direction in which the string moved which way the workers wrote in their vote. They would scold or commend them accordingly, threatening dismissal if they did not vote Republican next time. To hold a Democratic party meeting publicly in a plantation town was unheard of.

Intimidation tactics were rampant. One Nisei plantation worker active in Democratic party organizing—an activity for which he could have been fired—recalls holding his cell meetings on park benches in the evening, in groups never larger than four or five. Another organizer recalls using Morse code with his headlights on a lonely road at night to communicate a message to a fellow Democrat.

The labor revolution that was to break the power of the Republican party and of the Big Five came to Hawaii, as most things did, several decades after it had come to the mainland. But it played a larger role in transforming the fabric of Hawaiian society than it had in any other state or territory of the Union. The growth of Hawaii's labor movement was delayed both by the islands' isolation and by the racial divisions which the planters had so successfully effected among Hawaii's workers. For until the 1930's, most labor agitation in Hawaii had been organized on strictly racial lines. One of the last and most notorious of the racially organized strikes had been staged by Filipino workers in 1924 at Hanapepe, Kauai. There the police shot sixteen strikers to death, and sixty strikers were sentenced to four-year prison terms—an episode judiciously excluded from any tourist guidebook to this lovely seashore town. Prejudices which are still characteristic of Hawaii deterred any interracial union movement. The Japanese considered the Filipinos too ignorant to be organized. Portuguese workers shared the Japanese scorn of the Filipinos but looked with alarm upon Japanese aggressiveness. And hard-core organizers of all nationalities tended to look with some disdain upon the serenely unmilitant Polynesians. A labor leader and former Communist party member tells of his Communist colleagues' reaction when he tried to enlist a Polynesian-Hawaiian into the party in the 1930's: "If you gave that guy a bomb," he was told, "he'd forget it under a palm tree and go surfing."

It was on Hawaii's docks, where workers had constant contact with mainland seamen already skilled in union work, that the labor revolution began. The catalyst came in the form of Jack Hall, a tall, dour seaman who was a veteran of the 1934 maritime strike on the West Coast. Hall dropped off his ship in Honolulu many times from 1935 on, staying in Hawaii a few months at a time to spread unionism to the islands. He helped found Hawaii's first labor newspaper, the *Voice of Labor*, which was run by a succession of seamen and exhorted the Hawaiians to forget their ethnic groups and unite on class lines instead. "Know your class," the motto was, "and be loyal to it." The first test of this new loyalty came in 1938, when a strike was called against the Inter-Island Steamship Company, which had the financial backing of Castle and Cooke. When Castle and Cooke brought in strikebreakers to take a ship to the seaport of Hilo, on the island of Hawaii, several hundred union pickets met the ship at the Hilo docks. The police opened fire on the union men after they sat down to protest against the strikebreakers. Fifty men were wounded, a few crippled for life. The event was referred to as "the Hilo massacre," and did much to radicalize Hawaii's workers. By 1941 Castle and Cooke was forced to sign a contract with the I.L.W.U. (International Longshoremen's and Warehousemen's Union), the first of its kind in the islands. Since the well-being of any island depends on a free flow of goods, one dockworkers' union was now in a position to paralyze Hawaii's economy at will.

The unionization of the plantations came next. World War II brought to Hawaii the stringencies of martial law and a surge in the cost of living accompanied by a freeze of wages. By the war's end, plantation workers were more eager than ever to unionize. By 1946 the ILWU had managed to get industry-wide contracts for all longshore, sugar and pineapple workers. The crucial confrontation which proved the unions' new class loyalty occurred later that year when some twenty-one thousand plantation workers walked off their jobs demanding higher wages. Management retaliated with a typical but now antiquated Hawaiian solution: they went to the Philippines to recruit six thousand men as strikebreakers, certain that the Filipinos' hatred of the Japanese occupation would prevent them from joining a union with a predominantly Japanese membership. The ILWU cannily outwitted the plan by making a deal with the Stewards' Union working on the Philippines-bound ship. The immigrant Filipinos were unionized even before they reached Hawaii. The cooks of the Stewards' Union worked with spectacular success in the boat's mess halls, rewarding the impoverished Filipinos with extra helpings of food when they signed the ILWU's union pledge. ILWU units in Hawaii welcomed the Filipinos with music, leis and luau picnics. In the strike which followed, the Filipinos stood steadfast with their fellow workers, notwithstanding the danger of being rebels in a new land. The success of the strike lay in its total interracialism.

It spelled the end of the Hawaiian managers' "divide and conquer" tactics. The ILWU's national director, Harry Bridges, who had spent much time organizing on the islands alongside Jack Hall, telegraphed congratulations to his Honolulu chapter with the message "Hawaii is no longer a feudal colony." By 1947 the ILWU claimed more than thirty thousand members in a territorial population of half a million.

Another proof of the Hawaii unions' amazing new strength was their ability to survive the Communist probes that spread to the islands in the wake of the McCarthy hearings. Beginning in the late 1940's, a string of defectors— mostly Nisei—from Hawaii's tiny Communist party testified in Washington about Communists or former Communists within the islands' labor unions. The number of party members in Hawaii had always been minuscule. According to a 1951 report by the Commission on Subversive Activities in the territory, there were no more than sixty Communist party members on Hawaii's waterfront, most of whom were nonresident seamen. And in 1947, when a Nisei member of the territory's Communist party cell publicly announced himself as its titular head, it was, as an observer put it, "like the periscope of a submarine raising itself and asking 'Where's the submarine?'" Nevertheless, the proportion of persons visited by the FBI in Hawaii during the 1950's is estimated to have been greater than in any state or territory of the nation. There was the lasting threat of the yellow peril—"the subversive, disloyal Japanese"—and the ideology of the Big Five could only be supportive of Joseph McCarthy. In 1951 six men and one woman were arrested in Honolulu on charges of subversion under the Smith Act. Jack Hall was among them. They were tried and found guilty, but by keeping their appeals alive the Hawaii Seven, as the group was called, were spared the five-year prison terms to which they had originally been sentenced. What was amazing throughout their trial was the unswerving loyalty of the rank-and-file workers to Jack Hall and the ILWU. In such a newly liberated society as Hawaii, Communist probes recalled the plantation intimidations of the recent past. When the Senate Judiciary Internal Security Subcommittee began its hearings in Hawaii in 1956, over three thousand members of the ILWU walked off their jobs in protest, although, as one unionist remarked, "Most of the boys don't know Communism from rheumatism." A typically tolerant Filipino worker said in pidgin at the beginning of the McCarthy days: "By'n by little communista, get mo' pay. If get plenty communista by'n by mo' pay."

Both the leadership and the rank and file of Hawaii's labor unions remain, to this day, remarkably more progressive and open-minded than they are anywhere on the mainland. The Hawaii chapter of the ILWU has protested the Vietnam war more vigorously than any local in the United States, and its leaders have been visible in several antiwar demonstrations held in Honolulu. At a convention of the Hawaii ILWU in 1968 a student leader who was asked to address the meeting appeared on the podium with an army deserter at his side. The convention was held at a time when thirty-seven A.W.O.L. soldiers, deserters from Hawaiian military bases, were receiving shelter from federal authorities in the sanctuary of a large Honolulu church. Although the union leaders later strongly criticized the student for not advising them of this surprise guest, the delegates heard the deserter speak out his antiwar views without protest—a show of tolerance hardly possible in any other part of the United States. In the 1968 Presidential elections Hawaii would provide a smaller turnout of votes for George Wallace—a bare one percent—than any other state in the Union.

A combination of tolerance and apathy, a capacity for quick forgiveness, have always pervaded the islands' politics. In 1966 Jack Hall, the most subversive radical of the previous decade, served on Honolulu's fashionable Aloha United Fund Drive with Republican Lowell Dillingham, Jr., whose family had recently been the arch-conservative enemies of the labor movement. And the memorial service to Jack Hall held in Honolulu after his death in January 1971, attended by every political and business leader of the islands, was tantamount to a state funeral.

Statehood had come more calmly to Hawaii than annexation, in spite of the striking repetition of racial arguments heard in the United States Congress. "What happened to the pristine virtues of the Roman Republic," asked Representative James Donovan of New York, a prominent opponent of statehood, "when it started to take in the Senator from Scythia, the Senator from Egypt, the Senator from Gaul? What happened to all the old-fashioned Roman morals and Roman integrity?" Another reason for the conservatives' opposition to statehood was based on the power of Hawaii's

ILWU. Representative John Pillion of New York argued that statehood for Hawaii was a Soviet plot, and that the Communist-dominated ranks of Hawaii's labor unions were so strong that one was inviting "four Soviet agents to take seats in our Congress." Congressional opponents of statehood would have rejoiced if they had known the results of a large public opinion survey, cited by Lawrence Fuchs, which showed that only 43 percent of the islanders polled, and only 30 percent of Hawaiians and part-Hawaiians, favored immediate statehood. According to the poll, the Japanese were the only ethnic group in Hawaii overwhelmingly in favor of statehood, while antistatehood sentiments seemed centered on the islanders' hostility toward the Japanese. A part-Hawaiian stevedore said he favored independence because he did not want a Japanese governor. A Filipino barber correctly predicted that the Japanese politicians would take over Hawaii after statehood. "Who can tell what is behind those faces?" he queried. Nevertheless the statehood bill received its final ratification in the House of Representatives on March 12, 1959. Honolulu's offices and stores emptied out; church bells tolled; an American flag with fifty stars flew over Hawaii for the first time. And vast quantities of the popular island-made beer, Primo, were drunk in this former kingdom which now has one of the highest rates of beer consumption in the Union.

V

The metabolism of islands seems to be more vulnerable to change and encounter than any mainland place, to undergo more dizzyingly rapid transformations. There are few areas of the planet where the pendulum of history has swung more widely than in Hawaii. In the two decades following the end of World War II, Hawaii was transformed from an oppressed and semifeudal society to a progressive state which boasts the greatest racial equality, the highest union wages, the most efficient welfare system, the highest voter participation and the most liberal legislature of any state in the Union. In the 1960's, Hawaii's state legislature was the first to support Cesar Chavez's grape boycott, the first to provide for a state ombudsman, the first to pass a legalized abortion law (written by a devout Catholic Nisei with ten children, Vince Yano, and readily signed by an equally devout Catholic governor). It is also said to be the only legislature in the country ever to vote its state university more funds than the university had asked for—a sign of the extraordinary veneration for learning on the part of the Oriental groups which dominate Hawaii.

Few individuals have been more crucial in Hawaii's democratization than its present governor, John Burns. Burns was born into a poor white family, the son of an Army sergeant stationed in Honolulu. His reformist zeal was fired by his distrust of the islands' wealthy whites, and by his passionate admiration for Hawaii's Orientals. Brought up in the slums of Kalihi, a suburb of Honolulu, Burns had supported himself in his teens by working as a farmer in the grape fields of California, where he saw the effects of the depression on migrant workers. He began his political career as a patrolman in Honolulu's police department, and went on to head its espionage division and its vice squad. From the start this devout Irish Catholic cop, whose origins connote the most conservative traits of mainland character, has championed the causes of Hawaii's underprivileged, non-Caucasian groups. Tough, individualistic and vastly read, he is one of those maverick progressive Catholics, not unlike the Chicago labor priests of the thirties, who can quote at length from papal encyclicals on the sanctity of labor. John Burns has gone to daily Mass most of his life and ends all his letters with "May the Almighty be with you and yours always." But his thinking is often as unpredictably liberal as it is original. In the 1930's he was responsible for the regulation of Honolulu's brothels, which are noted for their ethnic variety. A Catholic priest had visited him in his office to chide him for his tolerance of the ancient vocation. "Ah, Father," John Burns had answered, "I don't pray for the abolition of it. I only wish that for every fornication there'd be a procreation, for then we'd all be golden."

John Burns's career has been shaped by the loyalty and support of Hawaii's Japanese. During the war he had distributed small favors to the demoralized Nisei, who, though not interned, were kept under close observation during the duration of martial law. In 1948, when he announced his candidacy for the post of territorial delegate to Washington, a one-armed veteran of the 442nd Battalion, Daniel Inouye, offered Burns his help. Inouye had come to visit Burns in a swell of disgust against the islands' racism. He had wished to join the Diamond Head post of the American Legion and had been turned away because the post was restricted to Caucasians. Over coffee, the two men planned the future of the Democratic party. They agreed that it could swamp the Republican oligarchy only by including a powerful contingent of Americans of Japanese ancestry. It was through the combined efforts of Burns, his protégé Daniel Inouye and a few other Nisei veterans that the 442nd Veterans Club became one of the most powerful forces in Hawaiian politics and that the Democratic party finally defeated the entrenched Republicans.

John Burns's road to power was slow. As a gruff, antisocial, teetotaling ex-cop who grumbled against "super patriots," hated ostentation, drove an old car, wore tattered clothes, distrusted any man who had not been reared in the slums or on hard plantation labor, Burns was not liked by most traditional Caucasian politicians. His political career was further slowed by his erstwhile independence from the ILWU, whose left wing he dissented from as much as he dissented from the oligarchy. In 1954 Burns's Democratic party won its first landslide and brought to the islands what 1933 had brought to the mainland—Hawaii's New Deal. The new Democratic regime doubled appropriations for welfare assistance and public school aid, vastly raised the state's minimum wage, unemployment and workmen's benefits, and placed tax burdens on higher-income groups. Burns was sent as delegate to Washington, where he became a foremost architect of the statehood bill, using totally unusual tactics. It had been the traditional strategy of statehood advocates to cautiously avoid references to Hawaii's non-Caucasians. Burns took the opposite course. He thrust the Japanese into the limelight, praising their war record, their political skill and their patriotism. "I told Congress that the really valuable people of Hawaii are the two-thirds who are not Caucasians," he recalled recently. "I told Congress that Hawaii's non-Caucasians were going to bring the U.S. a helluva lot more than the U.S. was going to bring to Hawaii." Burns's devotion to Hawaii's Orientals would prevail in every one of his actions. Upon being elected governor in 1962, he was asked to be an honorary member of the exclusive Pacific Club. He was the first Caucasian of any importance in Hawaii's history to refuse membership. He refused it on the grounds that the Pacific Club, for over a century, had excluded Orientals.

Burns's love for Hawaii's Orientals seems to border on obsession. Upon his reelection to the governorship in 1970, Burns chose a full-blooded Nisei, George Ariyoshi, as his running mate for lieutenant governor. It has been rumored that he intends to resign in midterm to make the impossible dream come true: to install a non-Caucasian as a governor of one of the United States. Burns has another dream. He was recently asked whether he thought that the racial prejudices of the mainlanders had abated enough to give Daniel Inouye a chance on a Vice Presidential ticket. "Yes," he answered. "Do you know why? Because it would assuage the Americans' guilt towards the colored people. Electing a Japanese, you see, would be going halfway."

Going halfway—creating a showcase melting-pot of races, seeing Daniel Inouye shake hands with James Eastland in the U.S. Senate—is the dream of Hawaii's liberals. Yet one senses that Burns and other Hawaiian progressives admire the Japanese because they are super-Americans, and exemplify values of self-discipline and the Calvinist work ethic. Burns seems to have less interest in the problem of the islands' original people. "Hawaiians," Burns answers softly when asked about the Polynesians' problems, his voice as tender as it is cynical. "Hawaiian life-style . . . fine if you want to be a beachcomber. Work *huki-pau* to go *ula-ula*. I too, when I was young, worked *huki-pau* to go *ula-ula*." *Huki-pau* implies getting one's work done as fast as possible. *Ula-ula*, in the governor's lingo, means to have a good time. "Burns always treats us," said a disgruntled young nationalist leader after a meeting with the governor, "like little Hawaiians." On the issue of the original Hawaiians, the most far-sighted men would tend to maintain their paternalism.

Most of Hawaii's changes occur in extremes. Under the leadership of John Burns, an alliance of the Democratic party and the ILWU now controls the islands as tightly as did the Republican Big Five in the first half of the century. In the 1968 Presidential elections, only two states of the Union, Massachusetts and Rhode Island, had a larger Democratic vote than Hawaii. Daniel Inouye was reelected to the Senate by a larger margin than any other candidate in the United States. In Hawaii's state legislature, the Democratic party rules with a 16-to-9 majority in the Senate and a 34-to-17 majority in the House. The only maverick exception in this Democratic stronghold is Republican Hiram Fong, who bailed the ILWU out of financial trouble years ago and has retained its loyalty ever since. For the ILWU is the gray eminence of Hawaiian politics. Made uniquely powerful and loyal by the common plantation background shared by its rank and file, it is said to have greater autonomy and influence than any other union local in the country. Its leaders present a very different image from the nattily dressed, limousine-riding labor leaders of the mainland. The ILWU's two top men, Robert McElrath and David Thompson, are plain-spoken but highly erudite former leftists, who dress in shirt sleeves and run a tight, efficient shop. "Hawaii's a small town, it's easy to know your people," McElrath says. "I'm not saying that we can elect anybody, but we can certainly defeat anybody or keep anyone from running. We asked Patsy Mink not to run for Senate against Hiram Fong this year and that's why she didn't run." Commenting on Hiram Fong's very narrow margin in his 1970 senatorial race against a recently arrived dark horse, McElrath made it clear that Fong had almost lost because he did not heed the ILWU's advice. "We told Hiram to run a low-key campaign, relax on his record, not come out swinging. We told him not to get into a peeing contest with that cunt of a newcomer."

By now the ILWU, the Democratic party and Governor John Burns—all notably more conservative after two decades in power—have the support of much big business on the island, and frequently accommodate the Dillingham Corporation, for instance, in its bids for dredging contracts. One of the islands' leading Republican politicians, Samuel P. King, descendant of a Massachusetts sailor who jumped ship in Honolulu in 1798, sees absolutely no hope for the Republican party to recapture its power. "We lost our power base when it became more profitable for big business to go with labor than to buck it," says King, whose father served for three terms as Republican governor of Hawaii. "The way they play ball here, there's an even greater collusion between labor and big business than there is on the mainland."

The transformations in Hawaii's big business, and the growth of the Big Five into large multinational corporations, have been as dramatic as any other change in Hawaii. Over half of the Big Five's revenues now comes from Pacific areas outside the state. Beginning in the 1950's, sugar and pineapple profits began to decline sharply, the result of vastly increased competition in the world market. The Big Five were faced with the problem of how to maintain profits in a place which might never provide any extensive manufacturing: the islands are deprived of natural resources (bauxite is their only indigenous mineral), burdened by high transportation costs, and have achieved some of the highest union wages in the world. Hawaii's businessmen, in that decade, looked to the mainland and even more to the underdeveloped countries of the Pacific to place their investments. Castle and Cooke, then the most aggressive and innovative of the firms, started the Big Five's process of diversification by buying out controlling ownership of Columbia River Packers, an Oregon canning firm, which was later renamed Bumble Bee Seafoods. It was the first time in Hawaiian history that a Hawaiian company had acquired majority ownership in a mainland interest. Castle and Cooke then proceeded to branch out into all areas of the Pacific. "We were all dressed up with a lot of money to go," explains Malcolm MacNaughton, who presides over Castle and Cooke on the twenty-second floor of a gleaming skyscraper in the heart of the Financial Plaza of the Pacific. "We saw Standard Fruit and Steamship Company on the horizon, the second biggest fruit company in the U.S.— we now own it entirely and our plantations in Honduras and Costa Rica have doubled in size. We have control over thirty-seven percent of the U.S. banana market. Our goal is to produce two hundred and fifty thousand tons of bananas a year in the Philippines. We also have sixty-one percent control of the largest flat-glass manufacturing in the Philippines. We have food-processing plants in South Korea, processing everything from kim chee cabbage to mushrooms, white peaches and tinned meats. We own mixed-concrete businesses in Singapore and have controlling ownership of galvanized steel pipe concerns in Bangkok. We have just bought twenty percent interest in a pineapple concern in Thailand . . ."

Castle and Cooke also controls 208,000 acres of Hawaii's land, and through its ownership of the Dole Pineapple Company, 40 percent of the United States' pineapple market. It owns the world's largest producer of macadamia nuts, and builds hotels and condominiums in various areas of the Pacific. Its ventures into underdeveloped Asian and Central

American nations where wages still hover around one dollar a day—as in Thailand and Malaysia—have helped it grow into a large international firm whose revenues have increased from some ten million in 1947 to over half a billion dollars in 1972. Only four thousand of Castle and Cooke's nineteen thousand shareholders are now living in Hawaii. The rest are mainlanders. It is a far cry from the acute fear of mainland encroachment which possessed the Big Five before World War II.

Amfac has diversified with equal vigor and still greater success. It is a service-oriented conglomerate, whose revenues—over a billion dollars in 1971—have tripled in the past five years. Amfac still owns 73,000 acres of Hawaiian land, holds long-term leases on an additional 94,000 acres, and produces one-fourth of Hawaii's sugar crop. Over the past decade it has also acquired the state's largest hotel chain (Island Holiday Resorts) and its most profitable retail-store group, Liberty House. Among its mainland assets are the Fred Harvey chain of restaurants, several pharmaceutical and electrical equipment concerns, several West Coast mortgage and consumer loan agencies, a dozen California hotels, and two retail groups—Joseph Magnin and Rhodes—which comprise some fifty stores.

Hawaii's trade with the Asian and Pacific countries has quintupled since statehood—the lion's share of it is with Japan—and these days its major financial decisions are just as likely to be made in Tokyo as in Honolulu. Henry Walker, Jr., the genial and brilliant president of Amfac, has an intense admiration for the Japanese, which is typical of many Hawaiian executives increasingly looking to that country for trade.

"No firm in Hawaii can function without being aware of what's going on in Japan," he says. "We're increasingly going into business ventures with them. They're so efficient it's depressing. They've invented a car battery so small they'll be producing the first electronic car. Toshiba has just patented a machine that might make mailmen obsolete . . . As for our own business boom, it's in good part created by our Japanese Hawaiian consumers. The Japanese ladies all have jobs, which gives Hawaii the largest woman working force in the nation and creates a great purchasing income. Oriental women have a tradition of working in plantations alongside their husbands or running the family store; they never had that Caucasian nonsense about woman's place being in the home. Thanks to them, Liberty House is the most profitable retail store in the country . . . The Orientals are more law-abiding than we are, so our stores have the lowest rates of shoplifting in the United States; the Japanese never go bankrupt, they pay their bills much more punctually than the *haoles;* they're our best security risk."

Walker's admiration is admixed with concrete plans for increased business with Japan, "particularly in the field of advanced consumerism—creative, distinguished know-how in all aspects of retailing, such as merchandise display." He predicts that Hawaii will provide a channel for consulting and wholesaling contracts with Japan: it has a lead over other states through Hawaii's numerous past dealings with Japanese firms, and the ethnic and linguistic ties that exist between Japanese and Japanese-Hawaiian businessmen. (Hawaii is also likely to be one of the largest and earliest recipients of Chinese goods, since its population includes over fifty-two thousand persons of part-Chinese descent—a special market for Chinese imports.)

Traditionally imbued with aggressive optimism, the islands' businessmen and politicians tend to have a grandiose, Messianic vision of Hawaii's role in the Pacific. There is much pompous talk in Honolulu about the twenty-first century being the century of the Pacific, with Honolulu at its nucleus. Some of Governor Burns's aides envision their state as the hub of business and banking for the countries on the perimeter of the Pacific Ocean—the Pacific Rim—within which Honolulu would become the Geneva of the Pacific, a center for multinational corporations that would lead to the establishment of an independent Pacific Stock Exchange. In this projection, Honolulu is seen as the center of heavy investment for the whole Pacific area; its commerce would focus on exporting skills and know-how to Pacific markets, its stock exchange would play an intermediary role between the financial markets of Tokyo, Hong Kong, Sydney, Singapore and San Francisco.

However inflated these ambitions may be, it is certain that Hawaii will continue to provide a spearhead for the United States' growing economic investments in Asia. Hawaiian businessmen have been most enterprising in exploiting the vast natural resources and the low wages of the underdeveloped countries bordering the Pacific Ocean. Over 160 Honolulu firms are already operating on the continent of Asia and elsewhere in the Pacific; Guam alone has some seventy Hawaiian firms. The Pacific Rim Strategy is a popular phrase in Honolulu. It was officially enunciated by Rudolph Peterson, a former president of the Bank of Hawaii and a director of the Dillingham Corporation, which has been one of the most aggressive of the Hawaiian firms expanding into the Pacific. "When I speak of the Pacific Rim," Peterson said in a 1968 speech to a California businessmen's group, "I am putting the broadest possible construction on the term—the western coasts of South America and of our own continent, and extending beyond Australia and the Far East to India. There is no more vast or rich area for resource development or trade growth in the world today than this immense region and it is virtually in our front yard . . . were we businessmen to play a more dramatic role in helping trade development in the Pacific Rim, we would have giant, hungry new markets for our products and vast new profit potential for our firms."

Castle and Cooke and the Dillingham Corporation exemplify the potentials of the Pacific Rim strategy; and Dillingham's remarkable stress on military contracts typifies the close alliance of financial investment and political influence in client countries of the United States. Dillingham has built water-treatment plants in Vietnam, condominiums and power plants in Korea, harbor facilities in Singapore, underwater pipelines and ship berths in Thailand; it has undertaken construction work in Guam and Micronesia, dredging operations in Colombia and Guatemala, mineral explorations in Malaysia, Thailand and Australia, and transport and construction work in New Zealand, New Guinea and Australia. In the Philippines it has built a multimillion-dollar steel mill and the Manila Hilton Hotel. Two of its recent contracts have been for a $140-million-dollar naval air base in Thailand and an equally large naval base in the Philippines.

"Follow the Hawaiian Way." A neocolonial, Big Brother attitude toward the underdeveloped people of the Pacific has grown among Hawaii's politicians and entrepreneurs. As Amfac begins to plan the first large resort complex in Fiji the Fiji Tourist Bureau is modeling itself on its Hawaiian counterpart. ("One, two, three, many Waikikis" is the ironic motto for Hawaii's impact on other Pacific islands.) The Bank of Hawaii already operates branches in Guam, Wake, Midway and three branches in Micronesia. The High Commissioner of Micronesia's Trust Territory is the former chairman of the Republican party of Hawaii, and its attorney general is a Hawaiian Nisei. Ramming its capital and administrative skills into fairly primitive island societies, Hawaii is helping to foster the very same ills brought to it by American capitalists for the past century: foreign control of the islands' industries and resources, erosion of their cultural and social fabric, the growth of tourism and the casting of local people into a servant class. The development of Micronesia and of other Pacific islands is Hawaii all over again. "The caste system is breaking down," says the manager of the Bank of Hawaii in Yap, Trust Territory, who still accepts ancient stone money as collateral for dollar loans. "The influx of Coast Guard and Seabees has brought widespread venereal disease. Guam, for instance, no longer has a culture. You can no longer find an old Guamanian song or dance. We take a Guamanian, yank him out from under his coconut tree, kick him in the ass and put him behind a desk for twenty years so that he can retire to sit under his coconut tree. It's crazy. How do you conceivably bring an individual through a hundred years of development in ten years?"

One of the most poignant evidences of Hawaii's disruptive impact on primitive Pacific islanders has been the recent influx of some twelve thousand Samoans into the state, the largest single migratory wave of the past decade. The vast presence of the American military in World War II created a desire for Western goods among Samoans, and they traveled to Hawaii—the nearest American place—in hopes of jobs, television sets and cars. Uprooted from their communal tribal ways in the slums of Honolulu, they are frequently arrested for petty larceny because of their failure to comprehend Western concepts of private property; and they constitute the second largest welfare-supported group in the state after the Polynesian Hawaiians.

Although it is inciting other Pacific islands to follow the Hawaiian way, Hawaii is suffering through an acute state of anxiety about the future of its own economy. This anxiety is caused by the fragile, fluctuating bases of the islands' income, which has been traditionally dependent on international decisions that are beyond its control. As Hawaii completes its transformation from a goods-producing to a service-oriented economy, the threat of total dependence on the military and on the unpredictable tourist business haunts many of its leaders. In a task force report prepared by a group of Hawaiian dignitaries for the "Governor's Conference on the Year 2000," held in Honolulu in 1970, there is a suggestion that

Hawaii's hotel business, vastly overbuilt and recently in decline, might get new life in the next decades by being turned into a "creative leisure industry." Adjusting itself to the prolonged leisure predicted for the society of the future, when citizens will take vacations lasting months or years, Hawaii's hotels could become "creative leisure complexes" staffed not by desk clerks or bellhops (whose functions will be automated) but by highly trained specialists in art, music or psychology recruited from the local university. Travelers would come for fun, sun and Hawaii's unique brand of pop culture. "The industry will be a magnet for students, professionals and government officials from all over the Pacific who will want to study it in order to build up their own industries back home," the report gushes. "Following the pattern set in Hawaii, other creative leisure complexes will be built throughout the Pacific, forming a Pacific or world-wide integrated leisure system with Hawaii as its operational headquarters."

An equally sinister projection made by a popular futurist at the University of Hawaii, which prides itself in its "futuristics" department, is that the fiftieth state could become a center for "retraining" or "retooling" lower-middle-class American workers in preparation for the future shock of the leisure age. The lower-middle class, Dr. James Dator suggests, could travel to Hawaii's creative leisure complexes to bathe away their traditional work ethic, become less heavily work-oriented and more able to enjoy themselves in the playland of the twenty-first century.

Another prediction for the year 2000 is that Hawaii could stabilize its economy by becoming a center for "clean industries," such as large insurance companies or legal firms specializing in multinational law, or for the same kind of "think industries" that cluster around the Boston or Palo Alto areas. And still another futuristic projection—the most ominous of all—is that of a vast Pacific educational community which would ultimately extend Hawaii's State Community College system to Samoa, Guam, the Trust Territory and other islands in Polynesia and Melanesia. In this scenario, based on economic anguish but pregnant with cultural imperialism, education would thus become Hawaii's major crop. Such an educational system would eventually include a trans-Pacific satellite educational network, based in Honolulu, which would provide multichannel audio-visual communication to all major educational centers throughout the Pacific basin. The network would enable telerama sets, equipped with self-contained satellite receivers and computer units and accompanied by a technician, to be flown or air-dropped to the most isolated island communities. "The portable telerama-computer unit and technician," the "Year 2000" report states in total earnestness, "may replace the hard-pressed and fast-disappearing missionary." Thus, in a sublime burst of electronic Messianism, Hawaii purports to spread the American gospel to the Pacific's most isolated atolls through prepackaged educational units. Its tentacles reaching into the vast Pacific Third World that is beginning to awaken to self-determination, Hawaii could become a very efficient bastion of intellectual and political counterinsurgency for the United States. In fact, a climate of counterinsurgency has already prevailed for a decade at the University of Hawaii's East-

West Center, a State Department-funded institution inaugurated with great fanfare by Lyndon B. Johnson. According to a study made by former East-West grantee John Witeck, programs contracted through the Center, in the years 1962 to 1967, trained over sixty Indonesian military and police officers—many of whom later helped to overthrow Sukarno —in small-arms use and "civic action."

It is ironic that Hawaii, which in the economic sense remains very much a colony of the United States, should have such grandiose colonial aspirations of its own, under the apparent rationale of "Do unto others as has been done unto you." Consoling themselves for their extreme isolation, Hawaiians have often fancied themselves to be the center of the Pacific community. The ambitions of Hawaii's elite are as vast and romantic as King Kalakaua's vision of a Pan-Pacific league with Honolulu at its center, and probably as unreal. For it is possible that Hawaii's tourist haven might soon be bypassed by Americans and Japanese seeking bra-less natives and more genuine South Seas oblivion in less spoiled Pacific islands. Even Fiji is a more likely location for multinational corporations than Hawaii because of its greater proximity to Pacific markets and lower cost of living. And Hawaii's hedonistic climate is not ripe for the think-tank industries, which have traditionally clustered near great universities like Harvard, M.I.T. and the University of California at Berkeley. The creation of similar institutions is a far-off Utopia for Hawaii, which still basks in the eighteenth-century notion that Pacific islands are blessed because they enable man and nature to achieve a perfect balance in the absence of civilization.

Alongside the aggressively expansionist attitude of the islands' new elite, there remains, among much of the white aristocracy, a great nostalgia for the quiet, provincial insularism of the old Hawaii. It is apt to express itself in the most outlandish forms of paternalism. An official of the Campbell Estates, a real estate trust which is the seventh largest private landowner in the islands, was recently asked what he missed the most about the good old days. "Well, in the old times we used to put a bottle of whiskey out on the window sill and the Hawaiians would serenade us well into the night," he answered dreamily. "Those good times are gone."

In 1931, Thalia Massie, the wife of an American naval officer, alleged that she had been attacked and raped on Ala Moana Road, near Waikiki, by five local dark-skinned youths. The young men—two Japanese, two Hawaiians and a Chinese-Hawaiian—were not convicted; the racially mixed Honolulu jury could not agree on a verdict. Although the testimony of Mrs. Massie, a notoriously unbalanced woman, was extremely confused and vague, a large segment of Hawaii's *haole* population was persuaded that the local boys were guilty. The case grew to have enormous racist overtones. The *Honolulu Advertiser* called them "fiends" who had kidnapped and maltreated "a white woman of refinement and culture." Many of Hawaii's whites were pleased when Thalia Massie's husband, in the company of her mother and two young American sailors, kidnapped and murdered one of the young Hawaiians while the youths were waiting for a new trial. Notwithstanding an eloquent defense by Clarence Darrow, Lieutenant Massie and his accomplices were found guilty of manslaughter, and were sentenced to ten years at hard labor. But they never went to jail. A few minutes after being sentenced they walked across the street to the offices of the governor of the territory, Lawrence Judd. There, under the pressure of the U.S. Navy's Pearl Harbor command, Governor Judd commuted the sentences from ten years to one hour, which the murderers served pleasantly in the custody of the high sheriff.

The Massie case would remain a symbol of the deep-seated racial tensions that exist in Hawaii's much-touted melting pot, and of the profound alienation between the islands' civilian and military populations. For Alfred T. Mahan's prediction that Hawaii would serve as the Gibraltar of the Pacific had come spectacularly true. Hawaii's Schofield Barracks was already the biggest Army post in the United States in the years between the two world wars when some fifteen to twenty thousand men remained stationed in Hawaii. In 1941 the Japanese confirmed Hawaii's strategic importance when they destroyed Pearl Harbor as their first objective. In the succeeding years Hawaii became the staging area for all U.S. operations in the Pacific, with more than half a million soldiers billeted there at the war's height. After the fall of China and the growth of the Cold War, Hawaii came to be the Pentagon of the Pacific as well as its Gibraltar. Defense expenditures in Hawaii doubled between 1950 and 1956, vastly exceeding the islands' income from sugar and pineapple exports, and became the number one item in its economy. In 1957 all Pacific armed forces were placed under one centralized command, CINCPAC (Commander in Chief, Pacific), which became the largest military command in the world, covering 40 percent of the planet's surface. It is at CINCPAC that some of the contingency plans for Vietnam disclosed by the Pentagon Papers were formulated. Having further increased in numbers since the beginning of the Vietnam war, the U.S. military today controls more than one-quarter of the land on the main island of Oahu; and it employs a greater amount of the civilian labor force (some 8 percent) than in any other state in the Union. One of the state's eight major islands, Kahoolawe—once arable and inhabited—is now a wasteland exclusively used for military bombing practice.

Another brutal consequence of the military presence, which is almost totally concentrated on overcrowded Oahu, is its impact on the housing shortage. More than one-sixth of Oahu's population—some 110,000 out of a census of some 630,000—are military personnel and their dependents. In 1969 only two-thirds of them were provided with military housing. The rest competed with Hawaii's low-income residents for public housing and rent subsidies. It is a source of great bitterness to the landless islanders that many recipients of the Hawaiian State Rent Program Aid have been mainland servicemen, while many local families have been left unprovided for. It is also a source of unease that the number of military is predicted to grow in Hawaii in the next few years as troops are withdrawn from Vietnam, Okinawa, and Korea. For if the United States' defense perimeter is pulled back from Asia, the fiftieth state might become an even more crucial forward post than it is now. As the inevitable fall-back point for Asian bases, Hawaii—along with Micronesia—will be on the front line of defense, a bastion of increased importance.

The enormous military presence in Hawaii is made all the more sinister by the fact that it is barely visible. Because of the traditional tensions symbolized by the Massie case and the high school gangs' Kill a Haole Day pranks, servicemen have been under orders since the time of Eisenhower's directive never to leave base in uniform. They have also been traditionally snubbed by the clannish *haole* elite, and they live in Hawaii in enormous military ghettos, playing golf at military country clubs, swimming at military beaches, buying their food at the PX's, sending their children to schools on base. Wandering through the honkytonk of Waikiki with their wives and children, they are indistinguishable from all the other crew-cut transients in pineapple-print shorts come to the islands on a holiday. "The military in our state," a young Hawaiian remarks, "is like the green slime in some science-fiction movie."

No state more clearly exemplifies Cold War fantasizing and the gigantic stranglehold of the military upon American society than Hawaii. Yet in few states is the consciousness of military domination less developed. Agitation against the military in Hawaii is restricted to a small fervent group of young radicals. For there is a great ambivalence in the islanders' feelings toward the military. Army personnel are snubbed by most, hated by some. But they are often one's employers, and are largely responsible for the enormous economic boom Hawaii has enjoyed for the last two decades. It is perhaps because of this ambivalence that the outstanding political issues in the state never focus on the military presence but lean instead on the problems of ecology, tourism and uncurbed growth. In the decade since statehood Hawaii's population has increased by 130 percent, and construction on the islands has nearly trebled. Honolulu's population, quadrupling since World War I, has grown more rapidly in the past fifty years than that of any other city in the nation with the exception of Miami. The population density of Oahu is greater than that of Japan. The number of tourists is predicted to rise to two million in 1972 if it continues to grow at its present rate. The numerous mainland firms developing the islands, and the eight major airline companies that serve Hawaii, recruit most of their executives from the mainland, and are in part responsible for the enormous flow of inmigration into the islands. Hawaii's boom, which is momentarily pausing, has brought some benefits: the lowest unemployment rate in the nation and an enormous increase in personal income. It has also brought the nation's most severe housing shortage, enormous increases in land prices, growing environmental pollution and the highest cost of living next to Alaska's. Housing prices have soared to 40 percent over the mainland average, and food prices 20 percent. Even a tin of Dole pineapple—grown and canned on the islands—costs a few cents more in Hawaii than it does on the mainland, which provides Hawaii with most of its fresh produce. There is some agitation on the part of the more progressive islanders to increase vegetable and fruit growing in the state. But the stranglehold of large corporations and trusts on the islands' scarce arable land—originated by the provisions of the Mahele and by the early concentration of acreage into vast sugar plantations—militates against any sizable diversification of crops. Such gigantic landowners as Amfac or the Bishop Estate inevitably profit more by encouraging the building of resort or residential complexes on their terrains, contributing to the increasing ravage of one of the world's most beautiful landscapes. The rape of any paradise is a melancholy prospect, and Hawaii still offers some of the most paradisial scenery on earth.

The dormant volcano at Haleakala, on the island of Maui, is a majestic bowl of copper, black and purple volcanic matter punctuated by monumental cinder cones. Traversed by swaths of clouds that alternate swiftly with a blinding sapphire sky, the crater's somber surface is speckled, in summer, with the gigantic violet flowers of the rare silversword plant. Twice as big as Manhattan island, lying in awesome stillness ten thousand feet above sea level, its air made dizzying by altitude, Haleakala crater was a place of pilgrimage for the ancient Hawaiians, a site for meditation and revelation. It retains the magic and sublime aura of the world's great sacred spaces: Delphi, Olympia, Chichen Itzá. Descending from Haleakala one crosses groves of the now rare, red-berried sandalwood tree, forests of pine and eucalyptus, vast grassy pasture lands, sienna-red pineapple fields pierced with the matte-bluish spikes of the growing fruit.

Hawaii's scenery is as varied as it is majestic. In eastern

Maui, in valleys of the Hana coast surmounted by tropical rain forests, emerald expanses of taro fields alternate in checker pattern with glistening rice paddies. Soaring waterfalls proliferate in these islands cleft by volcanic eruptions. Some are narrow, diaphanous, feminine effervescences of spume, others are broad and vigorously masculine torrents bounding out of dark ravines of black rock. They cascade into pools fringed with gigantic ferns, wild lantana, bamboo, mango, banana, pandanus, avocado and breadfruit trees, their vapor creating innumerable rainbows in air redolent with the fragrance of ginger and frangipani.

The big island of Hawaii is still being created, *natura naturans,* by the eruptions of Kilauea crater. The volcano erupts every few years, forging new coastlines, cloaking the island with miles of lava that solidifies into a brilliant, brittle crust of metallic blue-black hue. At Kilauea there are chains of bubbling, hissing craters exhaling clouds of sulfur, vast Dantesque landscapes laced with the vapors of the earth's belly. Walking through Hawaii's volcanic areas one is thrust back to the world's beginnings: Lichens, mosses, tree ferns— the planet's earliest vegetation—sprout from fields of lava barely cool to the touch and still pierced by vents of sizzling steam. From the edge of the volcano, fields of papaya trees and orchid-infested ferns stretch out to beaches of onyx-black volcanic sand fringed by treacherous, white-crested emerald surf. Hawaii's landscape is the most varied in the state, and the richest in historical memories. On its northeast coast, near the tender-green, cliff-surmounted Waipio valley, one can see waves breaking on the beaches where

Kamehameha I is said to have surfed as a child. To the west, on the hot and dry Kona coast, groves of fragrant, crimson-berried coffee trees stretch down to the cobalt bay where Captain Cook was killed, and where Opukahaia swam out to sea to begin his fateful Christian education on a New England ship. In the dusty plateau at Hawaii's center, under the peak of the perpetually snow-covered peak of Mauna Kea, cattle graze the pastures of the 186,000-acre Parker Ranch, the second largest cattle ranch in the United States, its lands originally granted by Kamehameha to one of his Caucasian advisers.

On Kauai, the "garden island," the tall and threatening cane fields are as vast as inland seas. On its roadless northern coast there are thousand-foot-high amethyst cliffs plummeting down to a sapphire ocean, cobalt cliffs plunging to viridian bays. The palm-fringed white sand beaches of Kauai's Hanalei coast are so paradisial that the producers of *South Pacific* could not find a better site to film their movie version. The grandiose three-thousand-foot-deep Waimea canyon, which changes from russet to violet according to the whims of the capricious Hawaiian sky, is fringed by groves of the scarlet-spiked *lehua* tree, sacred to Pele, goddess of volcanoes, a tree which many Hawaiians still dare not touch.

In its natural state the terrain of Oahu—the main island on which Honolulu is situated—is as superb as that of any of the wilder outer islands: a precipitously steep land whose rugged, lush, mist-swathed mountains recall Chinese landscape paintings of the Sung Dynasty. The city of Honolulu is glimmering with newness, its modern buildings standing like gigantic loaves of white sugar by the Pacific Ocean. Honolulu is still relatively unsmogged, untrafficked, and has a grace and ease of living not equaled in any other large American city. Its more pleasant areas are interspersed with tropical parks, laced with scents of tropical flowers and Oriental cooking, its wide and clean streets are filled with individuals of a dozen mixed races of great physical beauty. Children attend school in bare feet; and except in the homes of the more conservative white elite, visitors shed their shoes at their hosts' doorsteps, as in Japan. Separated from downtown by brief suburbs in the Tokyo-Mamaroneck style, the rain forest is ten minutes from the city's core, shimmering with rubber and monkeypod trees choked with giant philodendron vines, redolent with eucalyptus and guavas. It is a city where tension or bitterness are assuaged by Oriental courtesy and hidden by a floral curtain. Blankets of bougainvillaea and hibiscus shield the poverty of the Polynesian Hawaiians' ghettos at the city's edges. A float of the Washington, D.C., Capitol totally constituted of white chrysanthemums flanks platoons of parading marines at the yearly Aloha Week parade. Political candidates campaign in garlands of jasmine and carnations. And some former militants of Hawaii's labor movement—polite Nisei who were the nucleus of the islands' Communist party—have retired to run flower shops in Waikiki.

And yet one is seeing the waning of a dream, the increasing threat to paradise. Some of Oahu's scenery has become a nightmare of every institution the mainlander would come to Hawaii to avoid—sprawling concrete shopping centers, fried-chicken stands, hot-dog and hamburger palaces, drive-in theaters, automobile dumps, heaps of refuse washed up on beaches, foully polluted streams and shores. Forests of condominiums—mostly housing mainland executives and retired military—obstruct the view of Diamond Head from many areas of Honolulu. The greed of both local and mainland developers is at fault for the growing urban sprawl, with mainlanders taking the brunt of the responsibility. The outer islands, until recently in a virgin state, are not exempt from the rape tactics of entrepreneurs. On the west shore of the big island of Hawaii, the Rockefeller-owned Olohana Corporation is developing 12,000 acres of land into a sumptuous resort-residential complex. A few miles down the coast is the 31,000-acre resort being developed by another mainland firm, Boise Cascade. Signal Oil has leased 18,000 acres of Big Island land from the Bishop Estate for another resort, and has an option to buy 36,000 additional acres from the Parker Ranch. On Maui, beach resorts are being built by the Connecticut General Life Insurance Company. And on Kauai still another mainland firm, Eagle County Development Corporation, has started to develop 11,000 acres as a "total resort community." Like the other enterprises, it will be a complex of hotels, shopping centers and condominium apartments planned as vacation homes for wealthy mainlanders. Even Molokai, the wildest of the outer islands, famous for the work of Father Damien among the lepers, is not exempt from mainland encroachment. An Intercontinental Hotel is being built there; and the Louisiana Land Company has joined with the Castle-and-Cooke-owned Molokai Ranch to build a

6,800-acre resort with an option to purchase 43,000 additional acres.

Although much of the mainland capital is going to the neighbor islands because of their cheaper acreage, Oahu continues to be developed by mainland firms, notwithstanding the exorbitant price of its land. Connecticut General Insurance Corporation is one of the partners in building twin forty-story residential towers a few blocks away from the Ala Moana shopping center. Del Webb and Prudential Insurance Company are developing a resort area on Oahu's north shore, one of the few unspoiled areas of the island. Honolulu's monstrous new Ala Moana Hotel is a joint venture of American Airlines and the Dillingham Corporation, whose sky-blue construction cranes are referred to as "the state bird of Hawaii." The new Waikiki Beachcomber Hotel was built by United Airlines and Amfac. An estimated forty-five dollars out of every one hundred dollars earned by Hawaii's tourist industry go back to the mainland. Helpless in the face of mainland encroachment, Hawaii reaps all the disadvantages of statehood and pitifully few of its benefits. Ever since Captain Cook's time, the Hawaiian Islands have been singularly vulnerable to outside forces and incapable of combating their disastrous effects.

Should Hawaii follow its rate of expansion and become a society increasingly dependent on decisions made on the mainland? Or should tourism be curbed, inmigration limited, and more effective control established? An increasing number of islanders have lately been voicing the second opinion. Their fears center on the growth of pollution, an issue which has more explosive political potential in Hawaii than in any other state of the Union. In 1971 the publication of a report on pollution in Hawaii compiled by one of Nader's Raiders made headlines in Honolulu's papers nearly as large as those on the Sunday of Pearl Harbor. The report pointed out that most of the untreated sewage of Oahu was being dumped into the Pacific less than four miles from Waikiki Beach, spewing forth at the rate of some fifty-five million gallons a day. It made the blunt but accurate conclusion that Waikiki, where swimmers have been catching an increasing number of staphylococcus infections in the past year, is not safe any more. The only item of the report that thrilled Hawaii's environmentalists was its prediction that a decreasing number of tourists will desire to return to Hawaii, with visitors citing the overcommercialization and overcrowding of the islands, and their outlandish cost of living.

The state's tourist industry threatens to kill itself by its own growth, like some culture in a microbial jar. Hawaii's hotel complexes, planned with thoughtless optimism—"a monument to stupidity," as one Nisei state legislator calls them—are proving to be an extremely unstable part of the Hawaiian economy. Due in part to tenuous financial conditions on the mainland, Hawaii's hotels filled only a little over 60 percent of their rooms in 1971. The state's tourist industry would have faltered if it had not had the support of the military's R and R program, which is decreasing in scale with the withdrawal of troops from Vietnam. It is presently being rescued by the growing influx of Japanese tourists—some 270,000 are predicted in 1972 alone—who flock to Hawaii to sit politely on its beaches and reverently take pictures of Pearl Harbor.

In the past year a strong desire to restrict mainland encroachment has spread through all levels of Hawaiian society. Though not taken as a serious possibility, the radical motion for secession passed by Hawaii's Youth Congress has become a euphoric fantasy for some of the state's most conservative citizens; and the motto "Don't Visit Hawaii" is widely taken to heart.

"If I were elected governor," says Allen Wilcox, the aristocratic, part-Hawaiian president of the Big Five firm Alexander and Baldwin, "I'd put it on a plank to send everyone back who hasn't been here for fifteen years."

"If someone doesn't stop the military from retiring in Hawaii," grumbles a University of Hawaii historian, "in twenty years half of the state's population will be living in condominiums with German shepherds and armed guards in the foyer."

"It's impossible in a democracy," says Atherton Richards, a former president of Dole Pineapple Company and one of the doyens of Honolulu society, "to put those proper laws on restriction of tourism that you could have carried out in an oligarchy."

"Each time a tourist gets in my cab and says aloha," a Waikiki cabdriver roars, "I turn around and say 'And fuck you too.'"

Even the task force report on Governor Burns's Conference on the Year 2000 ended with a wishful prediction that the United States Congress might someday grant Hawaii special status as an "international state" with extraconstitutional privileges. The new resentment toward tourists and inmigrants was also expressed by an extremely select group of Honolulu society women who, upon being read the students' motion for secession, exclaimed, "Secede, secede, it's the only answer!" The group included a daughter-in-law of the three-term Republican governor and the wife of an executive of the Dillingham Corporation. They went on to lunch at the Hilton, discussing the delights of immigration quotas and limited tourist visas which secession would provide.

Hawaii's radical young nationalist movement, which began in the summer of 1970, is a strident, exaggerated version of a concern expressed by Hawaiians of all ages and ideologies. It is based not only on a powerful new sense of cultural identity and of economic deprivation, but also upon a grave ecological anxiety that may be typical of threatened islanders. In few places has the American ideal of unlimited growth, of an endlessly receding frontier, wrought more havoc than in Hawaii's narrow ecosystem. And the harm brought to these exquisite islands is not likely to be stopped short of drastic measures, such as inmigration laws and state energy-level legislation, or laws designed to limit and qualify speculative development, such as the one engineered by the remarkable young mayor of Hawaii island, Shunichi Kimura. After two decades of urbanization and internationalization, Hawaiians are entering a renewed cycle of insularism, guardedness and hostility toward the outside world. The Aloha spirit is facing extinction. It had been, in good part, an invention of the tourist trade, as false as its distortion of the complex Hawaiian character—which is mercurially intelligent, humorous but proud, aloof, circuitous and brooding.

The ecological obsessions that suffuse our fiftieth state have been called a case of "rock fever"—the semipsychiatric term which describes the claustrophobic anxiety some islanders suffer from being bounded by water. Anguished about the fragile metabolism of island resources, Hawaii's ecologists readily accept Paul Ehrlich's population-bomb theories, and their pessimism can become apocalyptic. Dr. Jan Newhouse, a popular professor of science at the University of Hawaii, starts taking his daily five-grain dosage of Valium at seven in the morning to allay his anxiety that the world, and most particularly Hawaii, will not make it by 1980. He foresees a world-wide famine in several years which will be accompanied by severe repressive measures and will turn the world into an armed camp. Newhouse, to insure his own survival, plans to leave soon for an island in the Pacific—he will not disclose which—where he has bought some meadow land. He has assembled an extensive survival kit, which includes essential medicines, birth control devices and rudimentary tools. Newhouse and his wife have voluntarily had their appendixes and gallstones removed, and all their teeth pulled, in order to prevent future need for these basic surgical processes. Newhouse is one of nine teaching fellows in science at the University of Hawaii who researched the problems of Hawaii's survival in the light of its fast-growing population rate. According to Newhouse, eight out of the nine scientists, in the course of their research, grew to need psychiatric care. The ninth, who resisted therapy, drove his car to the top of Mount Tantalus and smashed it to pieces with a sledge hammer. Their anxiety was caused by their conclusion that in the light of the general ecological crisis Hawaii was the very worst place to live. "There are three kinds of societies which have the best chance of survival," Newhouse explains. "Agrarian societies, those with low population densities, and those least dependent on the outside. Hawaii is devoid of all these qualifications. The food supply on this island is limited to about two weeks." Newhouse compares Hawaii's acute ecological anxiety to the adrenaline pumped into an animal by extreme surprise. "It would be hard to find any place on the planet that has changed faster in twenty years. Any organism is put into a state of shock by that rapid a change."

However legitimate, the environmental issue sadly obscures all other national or international problems in a society in which racial resentment is of a covert variety; in which the poverty of such underprivileged groups as the Polynesian Hawaiians is masked or assuaged by good climate and the availability of the sea; and to which the Vietnam war, though twice closer than it is to the mainland, has brought unprecedented prosperity. An A.W.O.L. soldier who had deserted from the R and R Center met for two nights in a row with several dozen intellectuals who were among the most progressive in the state. He announced his deserter's status in the middle of a heated debate on environmental control and Hawaii's ecological crisis. After his talk the group, which had been assembled to "do something" about the Vietnam war, immediately resumed its discussion of how to preserve

Hawaii's scenic splendor. There was neither anger nor sympathy for the deserter's plight—nothing but a flat disinterestedness, a combination of tolerance and apathy unique to this most amiable and complacent state of the Union. "I might as well have announced to an audience in Idaho," the soldier said, "that I had received a good conduct medal."

Only in Hawaii could the protest group with the most lasting political effect be called Save Our Surf (S.O.S. for short). S.O.S.—the bumper sticker seen most frequently on Hawaiian cars—is led by a Marxist-oriented surfer and body cultist, John Kelly, who has agitated for years with admirable stamina against the gradual closing off of public beaches by hotels and residential complexes. A demonstration of hundreds of barefoot, bikini-clad S.O.S. members at the state legislature, holding surfboards under their arms, is a totally normal occurrence in Honolulu. Kelly's slide show, which he has shown to tens of thousands of Hawaii residents, simplistically but triumphantly links the closing of beaches to capitalistic entrepreneurism, to the pollution caused by uncurbed profitmaking, to the imperialistic suppression of Polynesian culture, and to the Vietnam war. "Who do our beaches belong to?" John Kelly asks his acolytes after his slide show. "The people!" roars the extremely young audience (the Hawaiian surfer's median age is eighteen). "Who does the surf belong to?" "The people!" they roar again, as in a tribal catechism. And one out of eighty of them, if Kelly succeeds, might go on to picket against the Vietnam war. Issues of beach and surf, Kelly has found, might be the best way to politicize a society which, until the advent of a very grave threat, will remain profoundly hedonistic and provincial, a sugar-coated fortress, an autistic Eden, a plastic paradise in which the militarism and racism of the American empire are cloaked by a deceptive veil of sunshine and of flowers.

VI

On a sunny, hot afternoon in the winter of 1970, Kalani Ohelo and a tiny group of Hawaiian nationalists— some twenty of them—were picketing the state legislature in Honolulu to ask for more land for the Polynesians of Hawaii. Specifically, they were protesting the "rip-off" of Kalama Valley, one of the few places left on Oahu's south shore where Hawaiians could still make their living as small farmers—raising pigs, sheep or vegetables on small plots of leased land. Kalama Valley belongs to the Bishop Estate. It was being cleared to make way for a new 30,000-person housing development which, as the protesters stressed, would only serve the growing numbers of upper-income mainlanders settling in Honolulu. A few families had already been evicted from their homes in the valley. And the Bishop Estate, whose revenues had been willed to the well-being of the Hawaiian people, was threatening to bulldoze the homes of the remaining families. Kalani and his fellow protesters, who called themselves Kokua Kalama, "Help Kalama," had come to the legislature to see Governor Burns and ask for a moratorium on the Kalama housing development. The Kokua group carried signs which said *"Imua"* (Forward), "Hawaii For Hawaiians," and "Where Have All Our People Gone?"

The protesters received the same response they had received during their few previous protests. John Burns was busy, or away, and one of his aides, a polite Nisei in a bright floral shirt, had come down to say that the governor could not receive them. As the group disbanded, its oldest member, a resident of Kalama Valley, had clenched his fist and muttered, *"Imua Kamehameha!"* Kalani Ohelo had angrily shaken the old Hawaiian's shoulder and retorted, "No! Not Kamehameha! *Imua Liliuokalani!"*

The response was symbolic of the shift of consciousness that was making the new Hawaiian nationalism possible. The adulation of the demigod king, whose burial place remains unknown, was eroding. Kamehameha, to Kalani Ohelo's generation, was symbolic of the oppressive chiefly caste of ancient Hawaii who had been responsible for the white man's takeover. And Liliuokalani, who had drafted a constitution that would have restricted the vote to the Polynesian Hawaiians, was symbolic of her people's attempt to regain the islands. "Kamehameha, much honored by statues and holidays nowadays," Kalani Ohelo has written in an issue of the nationalist paper, "wasn't really fighting for his people. He was fighting the people for his own greed, so that he could rule Hawaii and make all of it his own domain, giving spoils to his haole military advisors. . . This unifying of rule later made it easier for land to be taken away from Hawaiians by phony 'maheles,' and eventually for the whole kingdom to be stolen by foreigners."

There was an instinctive historical revisionism in Kalani Ohelo's words, as there is in many other nationalist movements throughout the world. But what is unique in the

Polynesian Hawaiians' movement is that for the first time they were ceasing to blame the white man or the Orientals for their fate, as they had for the past century and a half. They were squarely putting the blame on the shoulders of their own ruling class: "It is our own chiefs who sold us down the river"; "The Maori chiefs stayed sober and fought back, and their people kept their lands." These were some of the comments frequently heard from the new nationalists. By ceasing to adulate their chiefs and their traditional heroes, by undertaking a class analysis for the first time, these young islanders were putting an end to the docile feudalism of their minds. In a sense, they were completing the abolition of the *kapu* and caste system that had been only half abolished in 1819. And by focusing on Hawaii's severe land problems the new nationalists were making an important Third World analysis of the state's power structure. Hawaii is a society whose racism tends to be obscured by the superficial racial equality and the relative power of some nonwhite groups— the wealthy Chinese, the politically dominant Japanese. But even such Oriental magnates as Hiram Fong and Chinn Ho are middlemen playing a colonized role for the white elite. It is the white elite, comprising a handful of corporations and trusts, which continues to have a monopoly on the state's land—and therefore on its true source of wealth and power. In the words of former Lieutenant Governor Tom Gill, a liberal Democrat who has long worked for land reform in the islands, "The basic problem is that centralized and concentrated control of land gives you both economic and political control in a society." The Big Five, after all, still control one-fifth of Hawaii's acreage. Hawaii's young nationalists are slowly helping the islanders to understand that the building of a truly humanitarian society in Hawaii, which has the potential of being the most humane society in the United States, would require measures as Draconian as those needed to preserve its environment: a radical overhauling of its tax structures as well as its zoning practices, a vigorous breaking up of the large landholdings, legislation providing for communally held land, massive reclaiming of military-controlled land for civilian use, and a much larger degree of independence from the mainland.

The nationalist movement will grow in numbers and in identity. It has adopted as one of its slogans a motto of the royalists who opposed Hawaii's annexation to the United States in 1893: "When the evil-hearted messenger comes with his greedy document of extortion, no one will fix a signature to the paper of the enemy." Kokua—which soon after its founding called itself Kokua Hawaii—has been active in pioneering ethnic-studies programs and community study groups in Hawaiian land problems. By reevaluating the events of Hawaiian history and reawakening interest in their islands' rich cultural heritage, Kokua has begun creating a new historical consciousness essential to any people's struggle for decolonization. In the school year of 1971–1972 some one thousand students signed up for the University of Hawaii's ethnic-studies course—triple the enrollment of the previous year—many of them in Hawaiian language and culture. And the Department of Education resumed teaching Hawaiiana in the state's public schools.

The new consciousness has begun to lead to political action. In 1971 Kokua had a large civil disobedience group of its own, the Kalama Valley 32, a group of citizens who had sat down in front of bulldozers to protest the eviction of the last residents of Kalama Valley. Kokua rallies now easily draw a few thousand people to demonstrate in the courtyard of Honolulu's state capitol. "Scores of legislators who watched from the three levels of balconies above," so the *Honolulu Advertiser* described one such rally with a typically Hawaiian sense of priorities, "heard demands outlined on ecology, surfing, the preservation of Hawaii and the Vietnam war."

A special issue of the *Hawaii Free People's Press*, a Kokua-supporting paper, bore the following dedication: "To all those people and institutions that made this issue necessary: Dillingham Corporation, Kaiser Hawaii-Kai Development Corporation, Aetna Life Insurance Company, Boise Cascade, and other rip-off artists; Sanford B. Dole, Charles Cooke, Samuel Damon, . . . the Committee of Public Safety . . . Governor John Burns, Captain James Cook, Tom Hamilton, and the Hawaii Visitors Bureau, Admiral McCain [Commander of the Pacific Fleet] . . . and other cruds who by their wanton acts define themselves as part of the problem." On the same page as this vituperative dedication there was another, which read: "To the Hawaiian People for their Beauty. To Kalama Valley for Its Innocence. To you dear reader, for within your soul and body, you have the power to right social wrongs."

Seeing the Janus-facedness of sweetness and fierceness in the Polynesian character and its tragic tendency to docility, it is hard to know how far any radical movement can spread in the islands. And however admirable its instincts, Kokua is sometimes hampered by its provincial politics of nostalgia, its simplistic yearning for the agricultural, tribal Hawaiian life-style of pre-Cook times. Most nationalist Third World movements have been based on an idealization of a historical past; but it would be hard to find a more extreme idealization of history than that held by some romantic Kokua members. Would these young nationalists have enjoyed living under the oppressive oligarchic *kapu* system of pre-Cook Hawaii? In Hawaii, as elsewhere, a cult of primitivism, a defensive and escapist attitude toward the challenges of modernity, seem to be essential to the struggle for decolonization. After a hundred and fifty years of cultural and spiritual castration at the hands of the missionary-merchant class, exaggerated ethnic pride and an extravagant romanticization of the tribal past is a sort of adolescence through which Hawaiians, like all colonized people, must go before achieving a regeneration of the ego.

An equally fervent nationalist group, also based on land problems, sprang up in the fiftieth state in 1970. It called itself, simply, The Hawaiians. It restricted itself specifically to the reform of a pitiful institution called the Hawaiian Homes Commission, HHC for short. The HHC had been established in 1920 by vote of the United States Congress. It had set aside some 200,000 acres of public lands for long-term rentals, at nominal prices, for persons with at least one-half Hawaiian blood. Although the HHC had been started in a spirit of homesteading—to redevelop independent farming and return the destitute Polynesian Hawaiian to the soil—it had become clear over the years that most of its lands were in areas so arid, dusty or steep that they were absolutely unsuitable for settlement. An official state report issued by the HHC's director states that only 2 percent of the lands assigned to it could be properly developed by individual farmers. And the white man's encroachment on the HHC's lands had begun soon after its existence had been signed into law. By the 1930's the HHC was leasing half its lands to American corporations or non-Hawaiian individuals—the military, sugar companies and pineapple growers among them. And Hawaiian families who qualified for a homesite waited six, ten, fifteen years for the land that was theirs by law. One family is on record as having waited twenty-seven years. It is to correct some of these ills that the organization called The Hawaiians—which grew to have a membership of some seven thousand islanders by 1972—addresses itself with language as nostalgic as Kokua's but more gentle. "We, the people of Hawaii Nei, have journeyed a long and dark road together," so one of its statements reads, "a road which grew smaller, rougher and more painful to us. It was only our spirit and love for our homeland, for our great mother Hawaii, that lightened the darkness like a flickering candle . . . Let us stop cursing the darkness of extinction, disunity and poverty. Let us each light a candle of love to help our homeland and our people . . . don't let us go back to being the SLEEPY HAWAIIANS." But even this most nationalist of island groups is not devoid of mainland influences. When asked how he came to start his movement, Pae Galdeira, the part-Portuguese, part-

Polynesian leader of The Hawaiians, looked sheepish and answered, "A *haole* mainlander suggested it. At first when he started pushing and prodding me to start this protest movement about our land I said to myself, 'Oh oh, here comes another *haole* trying to exploit me.' But as we got to talking I began to trust him, and he helped me to get confidence in myself, because that's what we Hawaiians need most: self-confidence."

One of the most ironic phenomena of Hawaii's last decade has been the arrival of the reverse missionaries: the progressive mainlanders who, instead of instilling docility as *haoles* had for a century and a half, are suddenly goading the Hawaiians to militancy and self-determination. And the new Hawaiian nationalism is a microcosm of some mainland movements of the 1960's, replete with the same ambivalence toward radical whites as was the mainland's black liberation movement. To what degree should one accept the help of the white radical, who brings in valuable skills and suggestions? To what degree should one exclude the white man, and build on ethnic pride and identity? Pae Galdeira's group began by restricting itself to the HHC issue, but has gone on to wider political action; it limits its membership to persons of Hawaiian blood, and is wary of Kokua Hawaii's Panther-style rhetoric. Kokua—which may be a transitory name within the chain of nationalist groups which will arise in the state—purged whites from its ranks in 1971. Based on a Third World rationale, it admits any non-Caucasian into its membership, and sometimes labels Galdeira's "Hawaiians" as Uncle Toms for shirking Third World ideology. (Uncle Tom-ism, in the islands, has a variety of appellations: a Polynesian Uncle Tom, like the mainland black, is called an Oreo for having a white man's soul under a brown skin; the Chinese Uncle Tom is labeled a Banana; and Uncle Tomosato is a Japanese.)

But the average Hawaiian has remained cautious and apolitical toward these new manifestations of militancy. He typifies the islander's avoidance of any divisive issue that might upset the unity of his tribe. He tends to look with cynical amusement upon any political activism, and with particular distrust upon Kokua's Third World ideology, which is difficult to grasp in a state where non-Caucasians— Japanese and Chinese—have token control over politics and finances. A black mainland radical, dressed to kill in skin-tight pants and black leather jacket, once addressed a group of Hawaiians on a beach about the need to join the Third World movement. "You must help to overthrow," he preached, "that white minority of the world who are oppressing you underprivileged nonwhites." The Hawaiians were lying about on the sand, looking gently amused. At the end of the mainlander's peroration one of them rose, handed him a bottle of Primo beer, and said, "Brudda, you're coming on just like those 1820 missionaries."

The Hawaiians have a parable about themselves: they say they are like crabs in a basket; as soon as one crab tries to climb out, the others pull him back in. The lack of professional achievement on the part of this brilliant and gifted people has puzzled observers of Hawaii for decades, as has their large degree of social deviation. For in past years some

40 percent of juvenile arrests, and a disproportionately high percentage of Hawaii's school dropouts and prisoners, have been of Polynesian or part-Polynesian blood. In 1969 the first scientific case study of the Polynesian Hawaiian was undertaken by a group of social anthropologists and published by the Bishop Museum. Called *Na Makamaka O Nanakuli*, it is a 148-page study of the town of Nanakuli, a lower-income community some twenty-five miles west of Honolulu. This report on the Hawaiians' life-style has drawn the same criticism from Hawaiians that Daniel Moynihan received from the mainland blacks when he published his study of the black family structure. But it was the first serious study of its kind and has triggered much reflection on the Polynesian Hawaiians' problems.

The Polynesian's lack of competitiveness and his desire to retain tribal harmony at the cost of all personal achievement are traced by psychologists to the earliest grades of school. Observing the study habits of Polynesian Hawaiian schoolchildren, researchers note that the only way to improve their performances was to grade them in groups of four or five. Whereas they made no effort to attain a high score for individual achievement, as would an Oriental or Caucasian child, the young Polynesians' performances soared when they were graded as a group.

The Polynesian Hawaiians' social cohesiveness has always been proverbial, as has been their love for young children ("I'm going to limit my family," the Hawaiian says, "I'm only going to have nine kids"). And the passion for children, the Nanakuli researchers note, makes Hawaiian parents much more permissive about their teenagers' sexual mores than any other group in the islands. In the Nanakuli community where the Bishop Museum report was researched, not a single woman was found who had not been pregnant at the time of marriage. Hawaiian girls tend to start dating steadily with one boy when they reach the age of fourteen, and to plan marriage when they learn they are pregnant. There is an amazing willingness on the part of Hawaiian males to marry young. ("Hawaiians can't stand being alone," as one girl explains, "and they don't have a career to look forward to anyway.") Parents tend to accept their daughter's pregnancy with great happiness. The prospective father often moves into his girlfriend's house. And the wedding, accompanied by the traditional luau, or feast, of roast pork, poi and much beer, is not necessarily performed before the child is born; it is just as likely to be timed in honor of a relative's birthday. Hawaiians' exultation at the prospect of another birth is ironic in the light of the state's highly progressive legalized abortion law. Hawaiians are the group most reluctant to use birth control methods or abortion, showing the deep instinctual drive of a race that has been much depleted. Hawaiians and part-Hawaiians have such a continuingly high rate of birth that some demographers predict they might again become the single largest ethnic group in the islands by 1980.

Hawaiians, anthropologists note, are the only twentieth-century people on record whose family size rises with their income. However large the size of their own family, Hawaiian parents increase it further through the islands' ancient *hanai* tradition of adopting the children of friends and relatives. Their adopted children are often given preferential treatment over natural children; and it is quite impossible to tell who the blood relations are in the tribal, radically antinuclear Hawaiian family. "This girl, my daughter, is my brother's child," says a woman talking about her adopted daughter. "Of course, my brother isn't really my brother, as he and I are adopted children of my father. I guess my father isn't really my father, is he? I know who my real mother is, but I don't like her and I never see her. My adopted brother is half Hawaiian and I am pure Hawaiian. We aren't really any blood relation, I guess, but I always think of him as my brother. I think maybe my adopted father is really my grandfather's brother. I am not sure, as we never asked much things."

In the sociologists' lingo, the Hawaiian adult continues—as he was in pre-Cook times—to be affiliation-oriented, as against achievement-oriented. He works in a spirit of helpfulness toward his community rather than from a desire for personal recognition or gain. He chooses to honor a commitment to a friend rather than benefit his own fortunes. (This character trait is the headache of the islands' banking firms: having signed a promissory note with a friend who goes bankrupt, the Hawaiian would rather go to jail with him than claim the money he is owed.) Whereas residents of Honolulu's Japanese district salute each other according to the delicate hierarchy of their motor-car status—the relative fashionableness of their Datsuns, Toyotás or Buicks—the Hawaiian tends to find greater pleasure in spending weeks remodeling

a 1958 Ford with his friends and relatives. Formidably powerful and skillful at handling machinery, the Hawaiian will put
out gigantic amounts of labor if he is allowed to work with
a group of peers and set his own pace. One of the most
interesting institutions of island life is the *huki pau,* or "work
together 'til you're finished," system pioneered by the garbage collectors' union, which is more than half Hawaiian.
Under its terms the workers are free as soon as they have
finished an assigned route, whatever number of hours they
may have put into it. Garbage in Hawaii is collected with
prodigious efficiency, neatness and speed. The garbage collectors are often through by noon, and think the rest of the
world is mad for working any other way.

Some months after the Nanakuli report was published,
one of the mainland psychologists who had authored it, Dr.
Ronald Gallimore, sat in his office, looking quizzical. "I can't
for the world figure out," he said, "what the Hawaiians
want." He paused for a second and added, "However, in a
few decades we may be on our knees begging the Hawaiians
to teach us how to live."

It is clear to readers of the Nanakuli report that what the
Hawaiians may want most is more of each other; and that
their refusal to compete in the white man's world with the
white man's tools has been their only way, to date, to retain
a Hawaiian identity which was threatened and scorned by
the white man's values and the white man's schools. It has
been their only way to resist total colonization. Never tainted
by the Calvinist work ethic, devoid of the individualistic
profit-making drives that have brought our world to the edge

137

of disaster, enjoying his leisure without guilt, living in tribal communes that have been traditional to him for centuries, the Hawaiian incorporates many of the contemporary values of the world's youth culture. He may be providing a prophetic clue for the way of life of the twenty-first century.

A quest for identity will continue to pervade the new Hawaiian nationalism. What does it mean to be Hawaiian in this ethnic alphabet soup that is our fiftieth state? There are fewer than eight thousand persons of pure Hawaiian blood left in the islands, but there are over one hundred and forty thousand who are part-Hawaiian. In a society where the original Polynesian stock has intermarried with so many other nationalities, Hawaiianness, like Jewishness, can be hidden or asserted, taken for granted or exploited with varying degrees of militancy. To be Hawaiian can be a choice, a sentiment, a sense of nostalgia, a set of values. In its more tragic instances, it has been a public relations venture, a night-club act. Those who take the latter course are referred to bitterly by the younger nationalists as instant Hawaiians, professional Hawaiians, or practicing Hawaiians. "One is born an Episcopalian but need not call himself one unless he practices it," a Hawaiian explains. "Some of the worst of us have chosen to be practicing Hawaiians." The practicing Hawaiian is usually one who has arrived in his vocation; there is a handful in each profession. He is held up to the society as an example that the Hawaiian *can* arrive, and is usually as conservative a man as can be found on the islands.

138

One such is Mònsignor Charles Kekumano, who holds a doctorate in theology from Catholic University in Washington, D.C., and is the leading Catholic prelate in the state. "There isn't one field of vocation," he says proudly, referring to a half dozen lawyers and doctors, "in which Hawaiians have not arrived." He is a member of Honolulu's Police Board, and sees Hawaii as "the last genuine bastion against Communism."

And there are professional Hawaiians like the Reverend Abraham Akaka, pastor of the Kawaiahao Church, founded by Hiram Bingham, who talks in his sermons about Operation Hawaiian Uplift, but spends much time blessing every institutional object on the islands—submarines, the latest hotel, the new shipment of tourist guidebooks received at Honolulu's bookstores. A famous photograph of Akaka shows him dressed in his black clerical bathing trunks, carrying the ashes of the great surfer Duke Kahanamoku to sea, a crucifix of two crossed surfboard motifs around his neck. In the past year Reverend Akaka has led a courageous but futile protest against the appointment of a Japanese Hawaiian, former Councilman Matsuo Takabuki, as a trustee of the Bishop Estate. It is typical of the Hawaiians' self-defeatism that they have submissively accepted, for almost a century, the governing of the Bishop Estate by the Caucasian elite, and that their present demands for a greater voice in the governing of the former crown lands have come decades too late. It is also typical of the islanders' subtle racism, and of the frequent irrationality of the new nationalism, that the Hawaiians should concentrate their frustration and rage concerning the Bishop Estate upon a trustee of Japanese descent. As shown in the character of many professional Hawaiians such as Akaka, the psychology of the victim, of the loser, is buttressed by a fatalistic, primitive, pietistic mystique that the Hawaiian people will be saved if they have enough faith. Akaka mourned the investiture of the new Japanese trustee of the Bishop Estate by ringing his church bell in protest. "The tolling of the bells," he said, "was a proclamation of our Hawaiians' people's faith in God, our stand against injustice and oppression of our Hawaiian people . . . our great hope is for the uplift of our people in the coming days and years."

There are other official native sons, such as Sammy Amalu, a Hawaiian jet-setter of a mixed princely line. Amalu makes his living writing a daily column for the *Honolulu Advertiser* laced with questions of genealogy, sometimes venturing into monstrously flag-waving "my country right or wrong" political diatribes. When faced with the question of the Hawaiian's low income, Amalu will retort that some part-Hawaiians—those who intermarried with the *haoles*—are the wealthiest men in the islands. Amalu's following is made so immense by the older Hawaiians' nostalgia for their chiefs, and for all genealogy, that he was given a hero's welcome when he returned to Honolulu in 1970 after serving his third jail sentence (his misdeeds had included fraud and passing bad checks). Upon returning from a stay in California's Folsom State Prison, he was met at the airport by throngs, and a special service was held for him at Akaka's historic Kawaiahao Church. A pathetic choice of heroes is implicit in the Hawaiians' dispossession.

Among the older generation, there is only a handful of brilliant and genuine Hawaiian nationalists, such as the writer John Dominis Holt, a kinsman of Queen Liliuokalani, whose life has been steeped in bitter nostalgia for the loss of Hawaiian culture. Holt, in the middle of an erudite discussion of Baudelaire's or Mayakovsky's poetry, will still throw his head back and chant the genealogy of his ancestors, stressing the fact that they were descended from the gods.

It has been said that Hawaiians are so concerned with where they came from that they do not know where they are going. One must look to more activist islanders for the uplift of the Polynesian Americans. And even some of the Establishment Hawaiians termed Uncle Toms by the young radicals are beginning to sense the need for this kind of activism. Myron Thompson, a Hawaiian sociologist who has served as Governor Burns's chief legislative aide, squarely accepts the facts of the Hawaiians' underachievement and talks as vituperatively as the radical youths about the fatal impact of the missionaries on his people: "Those cats who arrived here to destroy our culture are the same breed of cats who left England to have religious freedom. As for our chiefs, they're the ones who sold us down the river. As for our underachievement, it's because we have not been allowed to develop a sense of biculturalism. We've bought mainland education lock, stock and barrel. We'll become achievers again when we have developed school curricula that will develop the ethnic identity of Hawaiians."

Another indication of changing attitudes in the young generation is suggested by a teacher, Fred Cachola. Cachola, when he taught in the public school system, was one of five of the islands' 330 top educational officers to have Hawaiian blood. Like Thompson, Cachola believes that Hawaiian children are hampered by a mainland-oriented educational system based on competitive middle-class values that are as foreign to their ethos as they are to those of the Chicano or the Puerto Rican. In his own school, Cachola is trying to raise student performances by pioneering programs that will stress Hawaiian language and history and explore new modes of motivation. With all his fierce Hawaiianness, Cachola has an equally fierce nationalistic resistance to the violent tactics advocated by a fringe of the islands' young radicals. "If we resort to guns," he says, "we are playing the white man's game . . . it would mean that we are using the same tools that conquered us and that we have become totally assimilated."

But then, the majority of Hawaiians might prefer to remain assimilated, or oppressed, or ambivalent.

I once spent several hours with a Hawaiian in his forties descended from one of the islands' chiefly families. His family name means "the king who has no kingdom." His father, who was descended from one of Kamehameha's wives, had worked as a pipe fitter for most of his life. I was struck with the fact that Tom K. knew no folklore, no legends, no proverbs in the Hawaiian language other than the state motto inscribed on the façade of the Honolulu capitol: "The life of the land is preserved in righteousness." He had gone to the Kamehameha School, and reported that half of the classmates he remembers from his schooldays were in the police corps. The others were pipe fitters like his father, hotel valets, bartenders, heavy-construction workers, night-club bouncers. And yet he defended his old school. "It was like saltpeter," he said."We Hawaiians need that. We are sexier and more violent than the *haoles*. We need to be oppressed. Might makes right. It's the ineluctable course of history."

Tom typified the old Hawaii's secretly defiant but passive submissiveness to the white man. "My family brought me up," he said, "with the idea that you might as well not fight the *haole* system, or you'll be crushed. We prefer to defy your *haole* world in our inmost heart than succeed within it. You know our saying: 'No make ass.' Don't make a fool of yourself by rising to eminence or acting in any unusual way. Over the values of succeeding or acquiring or protesting, we Hawaiians have held the much higher value of maintaining the tightness and closeness of the family. As for our aggressions, we worked them out with such institutions as Kill a Haole Day. A gang of Kam students would go downtown and mug some American soldiers or sailors. Note that. Only military men. The *haoles* had imposed a military system on us and that's how we retaliated."

With a nostalgic gleam in his eye, he added, "It was very satisfying."

Tom was both radical and conservative; he was strangely self-contradictory, divided, apolitical. He admired Marxist leaders and reform Democrats but voted Republican because his parents had always done so. He was torn between the ethos of his parents' generation, who had rejected Hawai-

143

ianism, and the radical nostalgia of the young who desired it again. "I half wish I knew Hawaiian," he ventured. The contradictions, the cleavage, in him were shielded by his infinite decorum and courtesy, and revealed by the great sadness of his large dark eyes. Like other Hawaiians, he stressed the violence of his ancestors as if it were the only racial trait that could offer him an identity. "We Hawaiians are really a very violent race. There is this profound need in the Hawaiian to shed blood. The blood is not flowing enough these days." This was said with glowering eyes, the soft face attempting a resemblance to the masks of the war gods—the Hamlet assuming the disguise of the samurai. "We Hawaiians," he quipped, "are at our happiest when we are either oppressing, or being oppressed. It is just as well that you *haoles* are doing the oppressing now. You are less violent."

Tom was obsessed by the greatness of Japanese culture. He longed for the advent of the twenty-first century when—this was his prediction—the rest of the world would be taken over by the Japanese. In other words, he looked forward to the coming of new masters, of a new race of oppressors. In his view, the young Hawaiian nationalists like those of the Kokua group were idiots, the older ones were pretentious. "I refuse to be a practicing Hawaiian, or one of these new radical Hawaiians," he said.

"That's my solution," he added with a smile, "and that's also part of my problem."

I have a memory of Tom then diving into the sea and gamboling in it for hours, frolicking with an animal persistence and a religious veneration. He let himself be tossed and beaten by the surf, his black hair floating on the tide like that of a drowned man, and then he turned around again to court the waves, arms outstretched, with a kind of weary devotion, like a man making love to a woman for the sixth time. The vast Pacific ocean would always remain the islanders' great solace, escape and nourishment, the amniotic fluid that would keep them hedonistic and aloof, guarded, gentle and mysterious.

ABOUT THE AUTHOR

FRANCINE DU PLESSIX GRAY spent the first part of her childhood in Paris, and came to this country at the beginning of World War II. She attended the Spence School in New York City and Bryn Mawr College; she received her B.A. in philosophy from Barnard College, where she won the Putnam Creative Writing Award. From 1952 to 1954 she worked as a reporter for the United Press, and later for several French magazines.

Francine Gray has had stories published in *The New Yorker* and *Mademoiselle,* and interviews and articles in *Art in America* and *Vogue.* She is the author of *Divine Disobedience: Profiles in Catholic Radicalism,* which won a National Catholic Book Award in 1970. Her perceptive historical and political reporting for *The New York Review of Books* and *The New Yorker* has attracted considerable attention. Mrs. Gray lives in Warren, Connecticut, with her husband, the painter Cleve Gray, and their two young sons.